Math Expressions

Assessment Guide

Developed by
The Children's Math Worlds Research Project

PROJECT DIRECTOR AND AUTHOR
Dr. Karen C. Fuson

This material is based upon work supported by the
National Science Foundation
under Grant Numbers
ESI-9816320, REC-9806020, and RED-935373.

Any opinions, findings, and conclusions, or recommendations expressed in this material are those of the author and do not necessarily reflect the views of the National Science Foundation.

HOUGHTON MIFFLIN HARCOURT

Teacher Reviewers

Kindergarten
Patricia Stroh Sugiyama
Wilmette, Illinois

Barbara Wahle
Evanston, Illinois

Grade 1
Sandra Budson
Newton, Massachusetts

Janet Pecci
Chicago, Illinois

Megan Rees
Chicago, Illinois

Grade 2
Molly Dunn
Danvers, Massachusetts

Agnes Lesnick
Hillside, Illinois

Rita Soto
Chicago, Illinois

Grade 3
Jane Curran
Honesdale, Pennsylvania

Sandra Tucker
Chicago, Illinois

Grade 4
Sara Stoneberg Llibre
Chicago, Illinois

Sheri Roedel
Chicago, Illinois

Grade 5
Todd Atler
Chicago, Illinois

Leah Barry
Norfolk, Massachusetts

Credits

Cover art: (koala) © Royalty-Free/Corbis. (zebra) © Masahiro Iijima/Ardea London Ltd. (eucalyptus) © Victoria Pearson/Stone/Getty Images. (blocks) © HMCo./Richard Hutchings.

Illustrative art: Schawk, Inc.
Technical art: Schawk, Inc.

IMPORTANT NOTICE ABOUT COPYING PAGES WITH BLUE ANNOTATIONS
The blue annotations that appear in this book are printed in nonreproducible blue ink. These annotations should not appear when the pages are copied on a normal setting. Some machines may need to be adjusted to a lighter setting so that the annotations do not appear. The annotations most likely will show when the pages are copied on a dark setting.

Printed in the U.S.A.

ISBN: 978-0-547-06700-1

3 4 5 6 7 8 9 EB 17 16 15 14 13 12 11 10 09

TABLE OF CONTENTS

Class Record Sheet
Beginning of Year Inventory

Name of Student	Number and Operations		Algebra		Geometry		Measurement		Data Analysis	

Grade 1 Inventory Test Correlation

Inventory Test Item	NCTM Standard	GK Unit Learning Goals
1–2	Number and Operations	K.1.3
3–6	Number and Operations	K.1.1, K.1.4
7–8	Number and Operations	K.2.3, K.3.2
9–10	Number and Operations	K.1.4, K.2.2
11	Number and Operations	K.1.1, K.2.1
12–13	Number and Operations	K.4.5
14–15	Number and Operations	K.6.1
16–17	Number and Operations	K.3.1, K.4.1, K.5.3
18–19	Number and Operations	K.4.2, K.5.2
20	Number and Operations	K.3.4, K.4.4
21–23	Number and Operations	K.4.3
24–25	Number and Operations	K.5.6
26–27	Algebra	K.3.5
28	Algebra	K.5.5
29–32	Algebra	K.2.4, K.3.3, K.4.6, K.5.1
33–34	Geometry	K.2.5
35	Geometry	K.2.5
36–37	Geometry	K.2.5
38	Measurement	K.6.3
39	Measurement	K.6.4
40	Measurement	K.6.5
41–43	Measurement	K.6.2
44–46	Data Analysis and Probability	K.4.5
47–50	Data Analysis and Probability	K.4.5

Name

Number and Operations

Exercises 1–2. Draw.

Draw 4 squares.	Draw 2 triangles.
Check children's drawings.	Check children's drawings.

Exercises 3–6. How many bananas? Write the number.

7

1

10

5

Exercises 7–8. Draw circles to show the number. Use a 5-group.

6

8

Name

Exercises 9–10. Write the numbers.

Write the number 5.

5

Write the number 10.

10

Exercise 11. Ring the groups of 6. X out groups that are not 6.

6

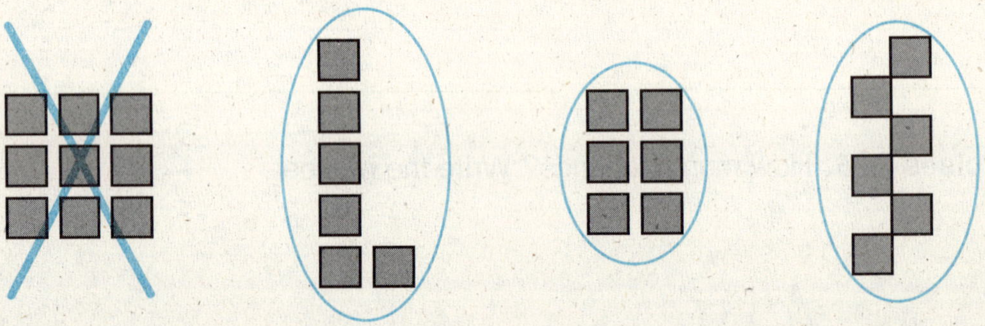

Exercises 12–13. Count and write how many. Ring fewer.

Exercises 14–15. Write the letter and value for each coin.

Penny = P Nickel = N Dime = D

P 1¢

D 10¢

Name ______________________________

Exercises 16–17. Write the partners.

5

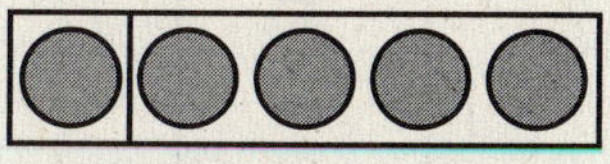

1 + 4

5

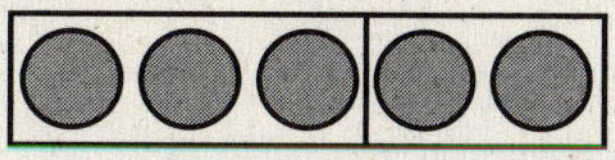

3 + 2

5

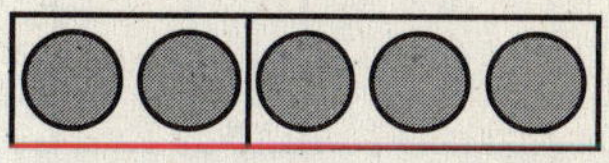

2 + 3

8

3 + 5

8

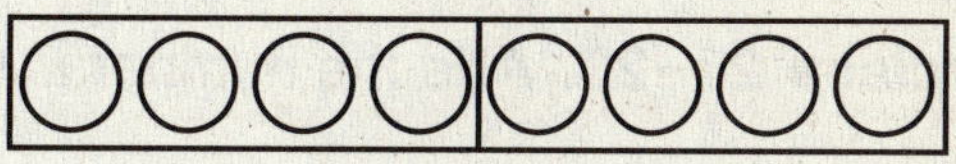

4 + 4

Exercises 18–19. Show the teen number as ten and extra ones.
Draw circles. Then complete the equation.

15

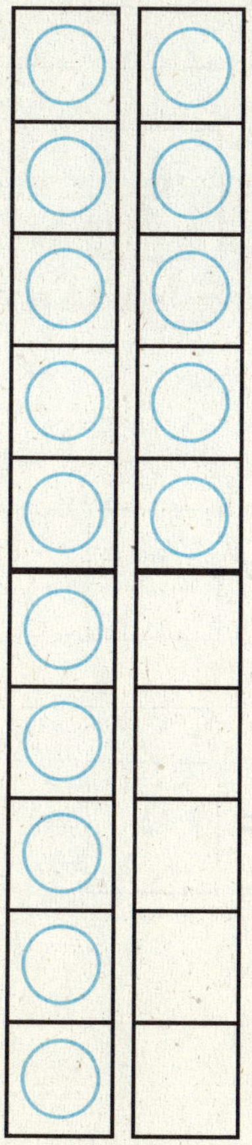

10 + 5 = 15

18

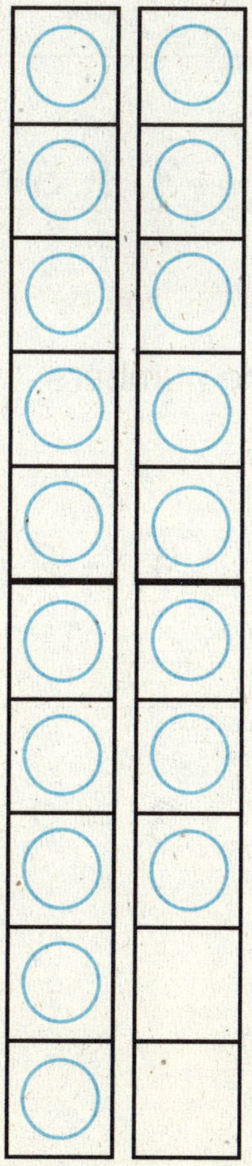

10 + 8 = 18

Name

Exercises 20. Write the numbers 1 through 30.

1	2	3	4	5	6	7	8	9	10
11	12	13	14	15	16	17	18	19	20
21	22	23	24	25	26	27	28	29	30

Exercises 21–23. Add the numbers.

4 + 1 = 5   5 + 1 = 6   6 + 1 = 7

5 + 5 = 10   6 + 2 = 8   2 + 5 = 7

7 + 2 = 9   3 + 6 = 9   4 + 4 = 8

Exercises 24–25. Subtract the numbers.

5 − 5 = 0   4 − 2 = 2   5 − 2 = 3

3 − 1 = 2   3 − 2 = 1   4 − 0 = 4

Name

Algebra

Exercises 26–27. Write each number and = or ≠.

5 = 5

9 ≠ 7

Exercise 28. Add (draw more) to make the two groups equal.
Write the number and the partners.

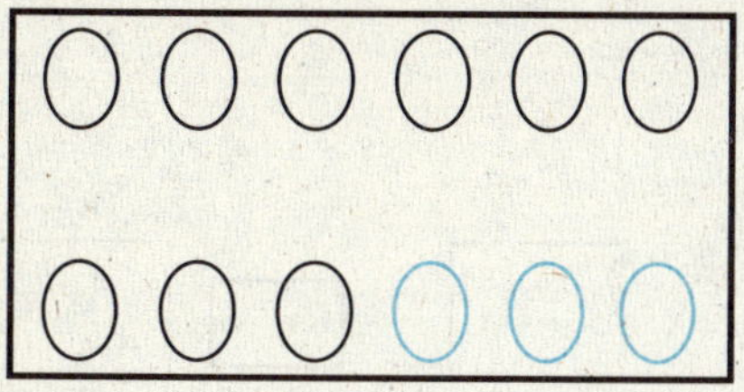

6

3+3

Exercises 29–32. Continue the pattern.

△	○	△	○	△	○	△	○	△	○	△	○

A	C	C	A	C	C	A	C	C	A	C	C

□	□	□	◇	□	□	□	◇	□	□	□	◇

1	1	3	1	1	3	1	1	3	1	1	3

Name

Geometry

Exercises 33–34. Draw a side of the shape.

Children will draw
a rectangle or a square.

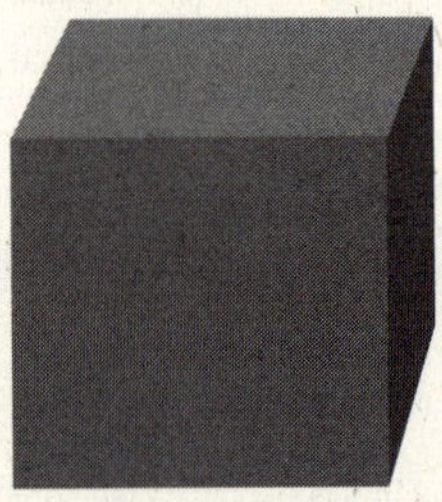

Children will draw
a square.

Exercise 35. Color all of the shapes of one kind in the same color. Count the number of each shape in the picture. Write the number.

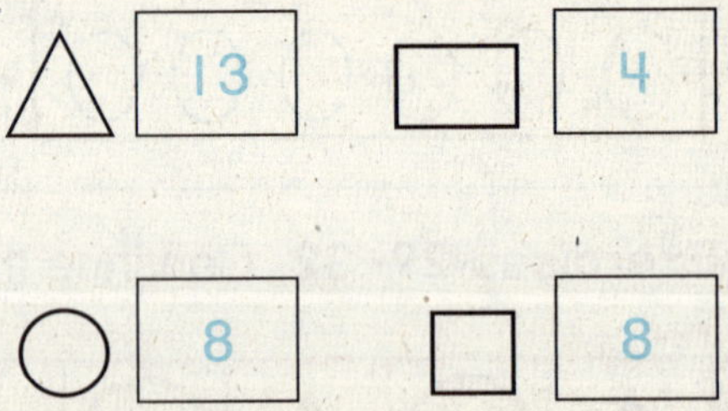

Exercises 36–37. Draw the shape. Sample answers shown.

3 corners and 3 sides

curved and no corners

Name

Measurement

Exercise 38. Use square-inch tiles to measure the length. How many inches?

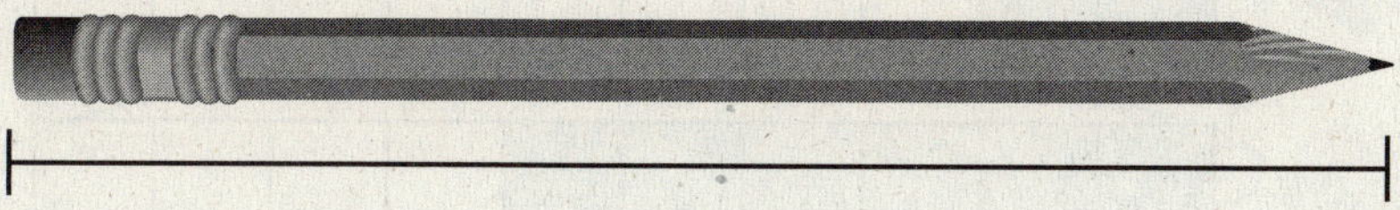

4 inches

Exercise 39. Use your centimeter cubes to measure the length. How many centimeters?

8 cm

Exercise 40. Write how many centimeters. Ring the longer row.

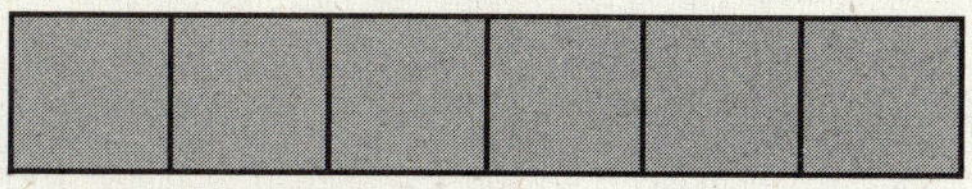

6 cm

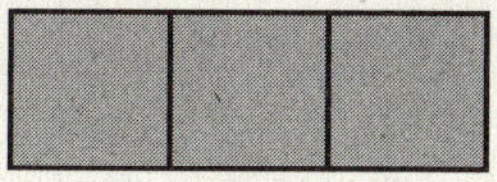

3 cm

Exercises 41–43. Read the clock. Write the time on the digital clock.

6:00

hour : minute

4:00

hour : minute

10:00

hour : minute

Name

Data Analysis

Exercises 44–46. Color the graph. Show how many fish of each kind are in the tank.

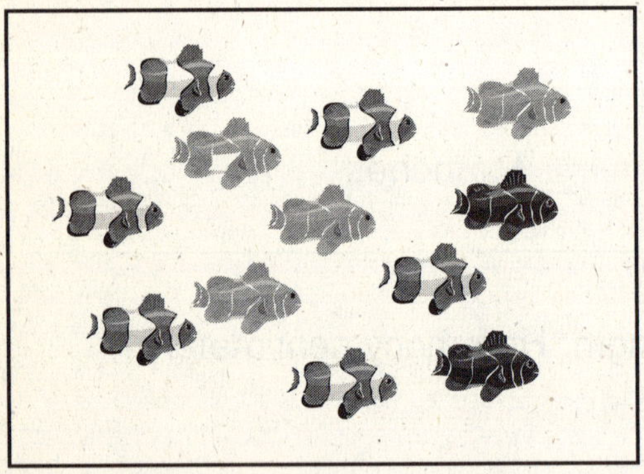

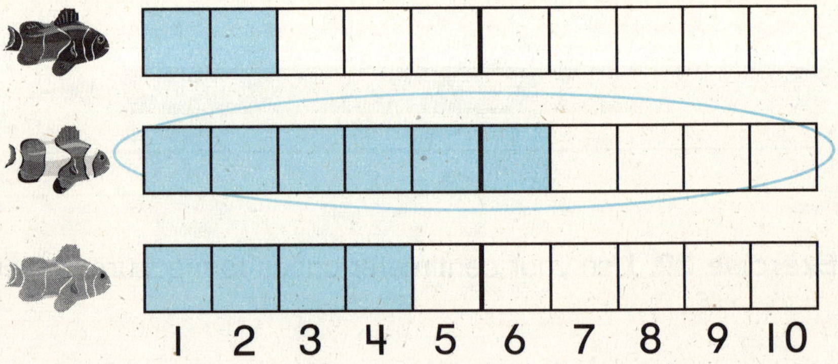

How many of each kind of fish are in the tank? Write the number.

 4

 6

 2

Ring the row with the most fish.

Exercises 47–50. Color the graph. Show how many apples and oranges are in the box.

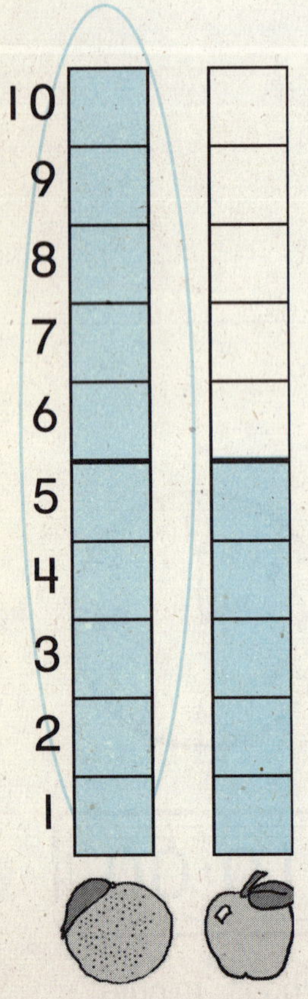

How many apples are in the box? 5

How many oranges are in the box? 10

Ring the column with more.

Class Record Sheet

Unit _____

Name of Student	Unit Objectives								

Unit 1
Quick Quiz 1

Name ____________________

Repeat the pattern.

1. 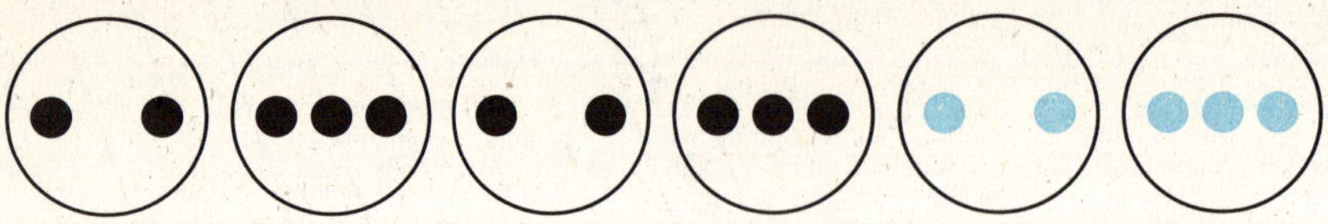

---

2. Write number 5.

5

3. Write number 3.

3

4. How many dogs? Write the number in the box.

2

5. How many triangles? Write the number in the box.

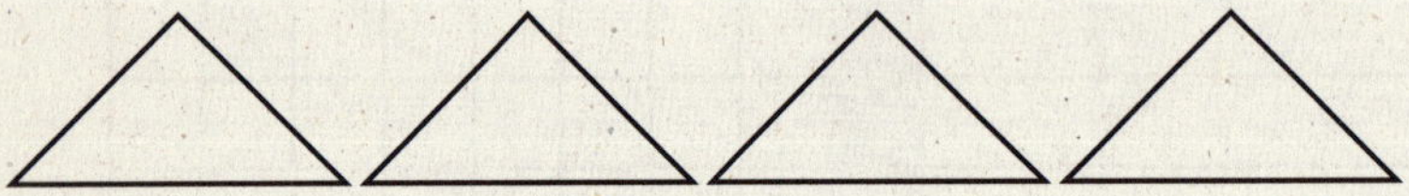

4

Unit 1
Quick Quiz 2

Name ______________________________

1. Write number 9.

9

Draw a break-apart line. Color the circles to show the 5-partners. Write the partners and the switched partners.

2. 

1 + 4 and 4 + 1

3. 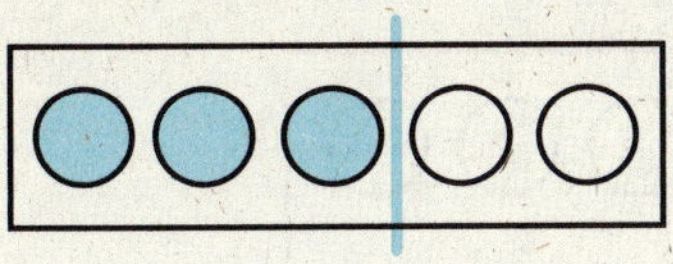

3 + 2 and 2 + 3

Draw the rest of the dots in the empty box.

4. 7

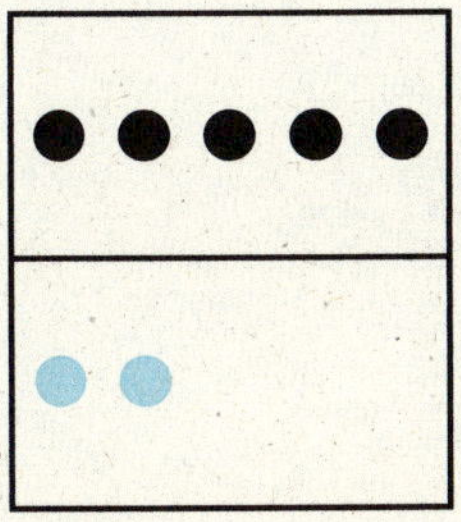

5. 9

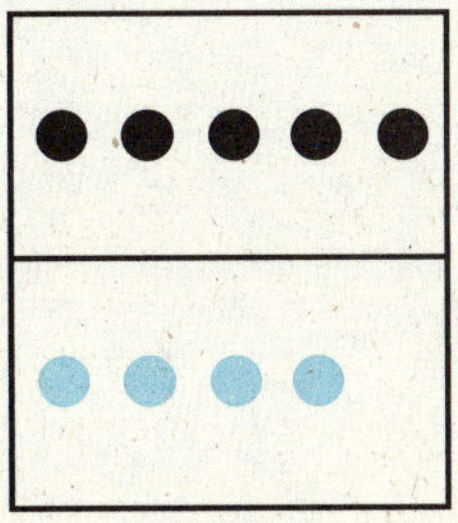

Unit 1
Quick Quiz 3

Name ____________________

Draw the rest of the dots in the empty box.

1. 8

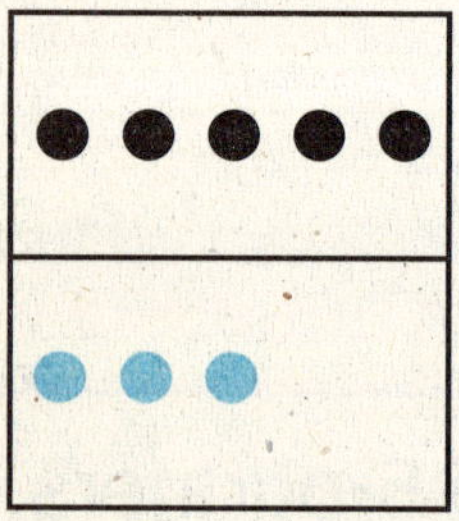

2. 10

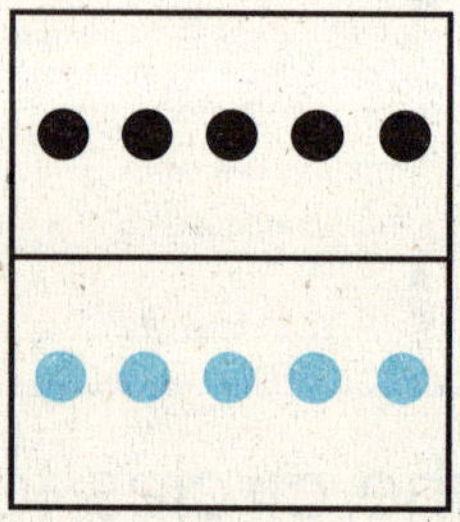

3. 6

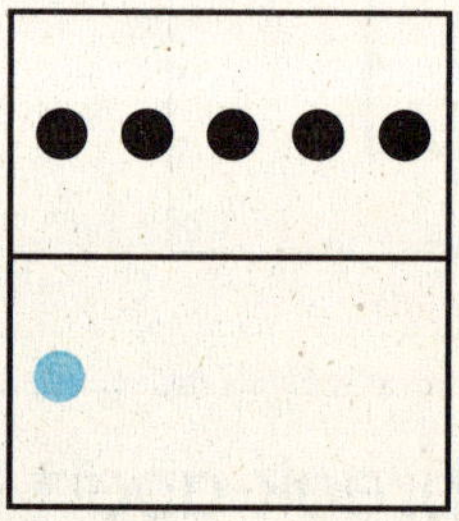

Odd or even? Ring one.

4.

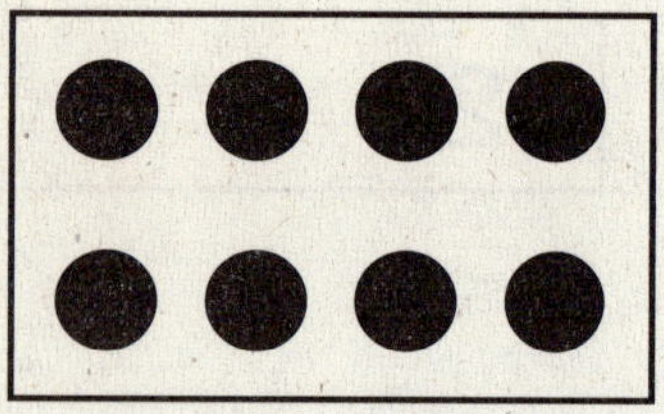

odd even

5.

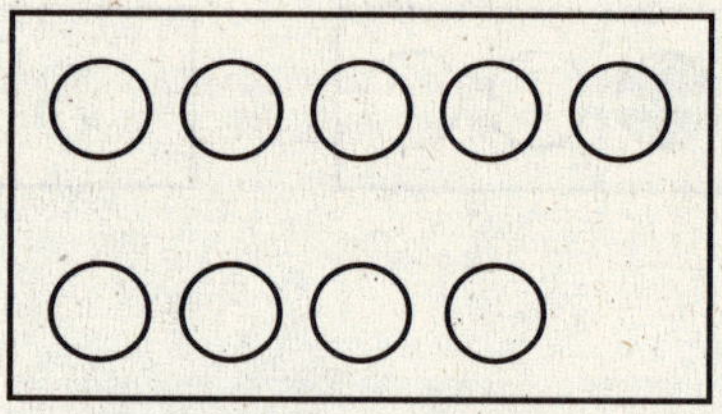

odd even

Unit 1 Test Form A

Name ______________________________

Repeat the patterns.

1. 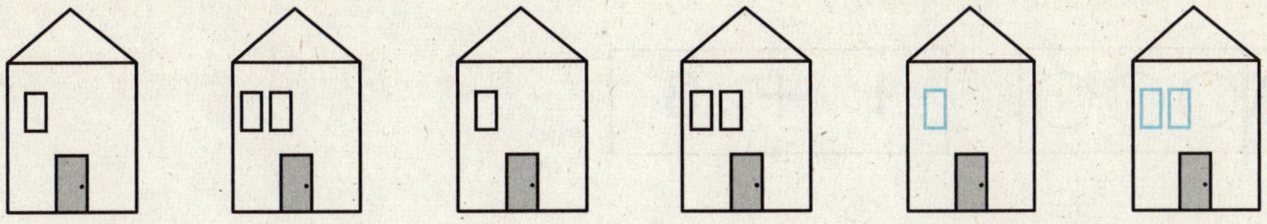

2.

−	+	+	−	+	+	−	+	+	−	+	+	−	+	+

3.

2	3	4	2	3	4	2	3	4	2	3	4	2	3	4

4. Write number 4.

4

5. Write number 6.

6

6. Write number 3.

3

7. Write number 9.

9

8. How many turtles? Write the number in the box.

6

9. How many trees? Write the number in the box.

4

Name

Draw the break-apart line. Color the circles to show the 4-partners.
Write the partners.

10.  1 + 3

11. 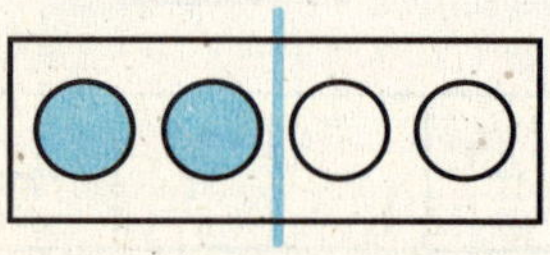 2 + 2

Show the 6-partners and the switched partners.

12.  1 + 5 and 5 + 1

13.  2 + 4 and 4 + 2

14. 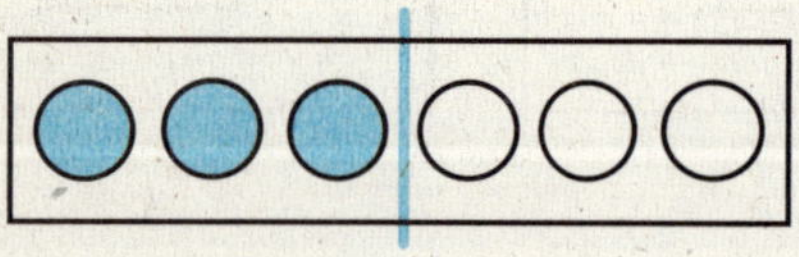 3 + 3 and 3 + 3

Draw the rest of the dots in the empty box.

15. 10

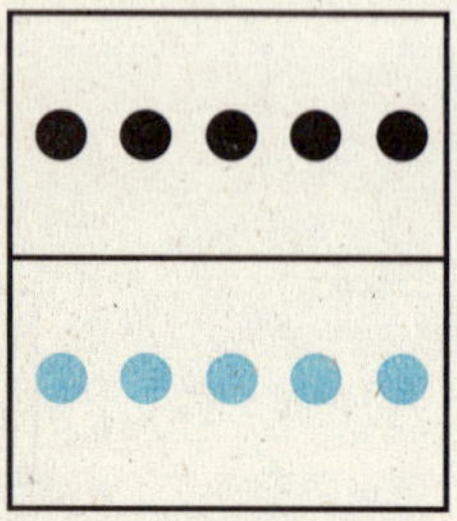

16. 6

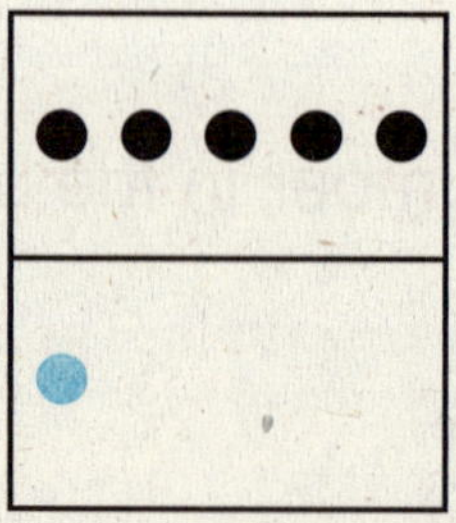

17. 8

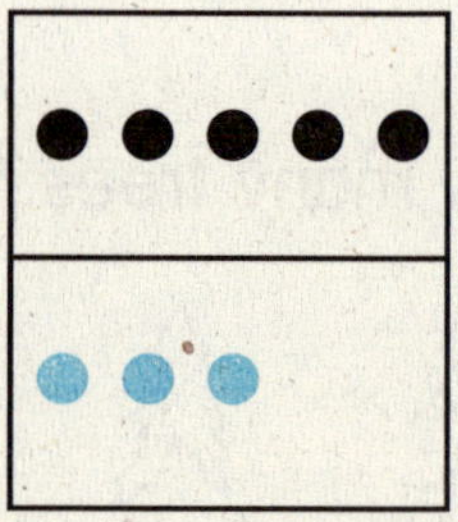

Name

Odd or even? Ring one.

18.

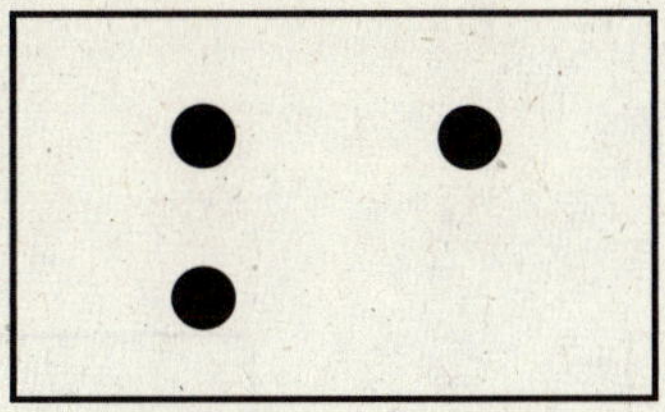

odd even

19.

odd even

20. Extended Response Draw 2 ways to show 2 circles and 3 squares. Check children's drawings. Sample answers are shown.

*Item 20 also assesses the Process Skills of Reasoning and Representation.

Unit 1 Test
Form B

Name ______________________________

Fill in the ○ for the correct answer.

What comes next in the pattern?

1.

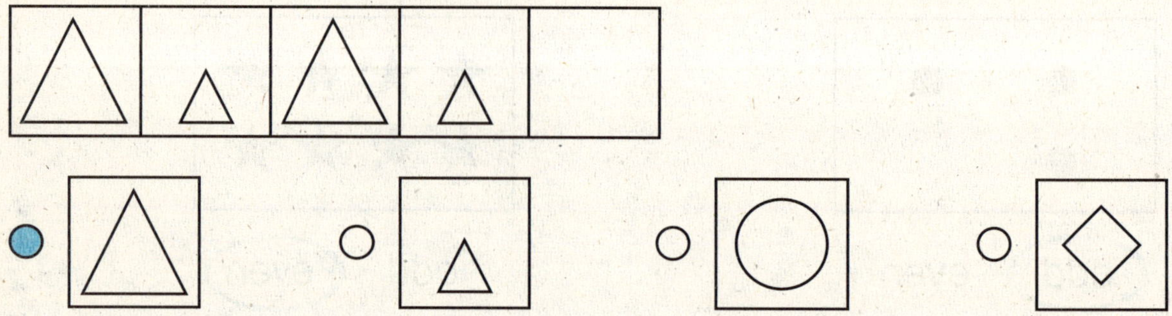

2.

+	−	−	+	−	−	+	−	−	+	

● − ○ + + ○ + ○ ●

3.

3	4	5	3	4	5	3	4	5	

○ 6 ○ 5 ○ 4 ● 3

Which number is made correctly?

4.

5.

6.

7.

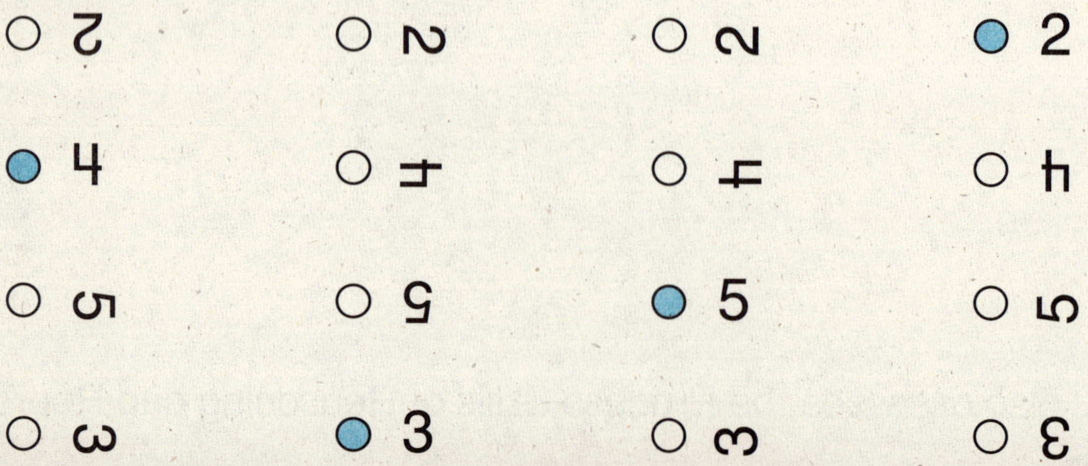

Name

8. How many airplanes?

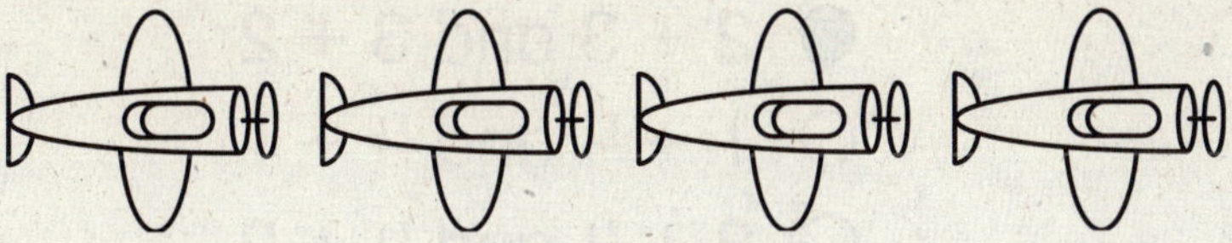

○ 2 ○ 3 ● 4 ○ 5

9. How many trees?

○ 2 ○ 3 ○ 4 ● 5

Look at the break-apart line. What are the 4-partners?

10. 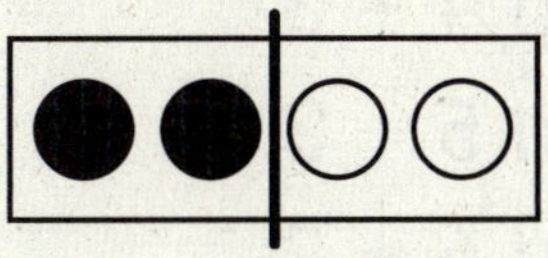

● 2 + 2 ○ 1 + 3 ○ 3 + 1 ○ 2 + 1

11. 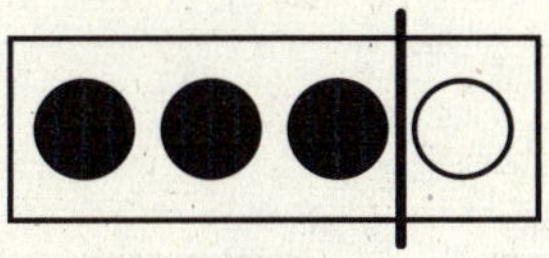

○ 1 + 4 ○ 2 + 2 ● 3 + 1 ○ 3 + 2

Name ______________________________

12. Which shows the 5-partners and the switched partners?

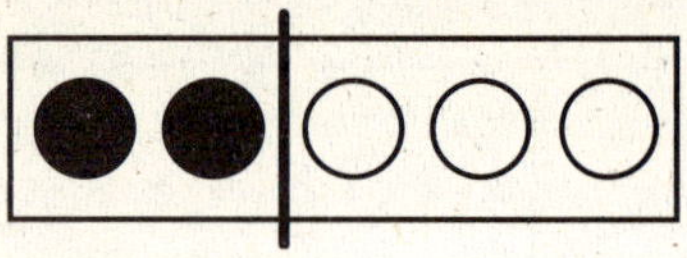

- ● 2 + 3 and 3 + 2
- ○ 1 + 4 and 4 + 1
- ○ 2 + 4 and 4 + 2
- ○ 5 + 1 and 1 + 5

13. Which shows the 9-partners and the switched partners?

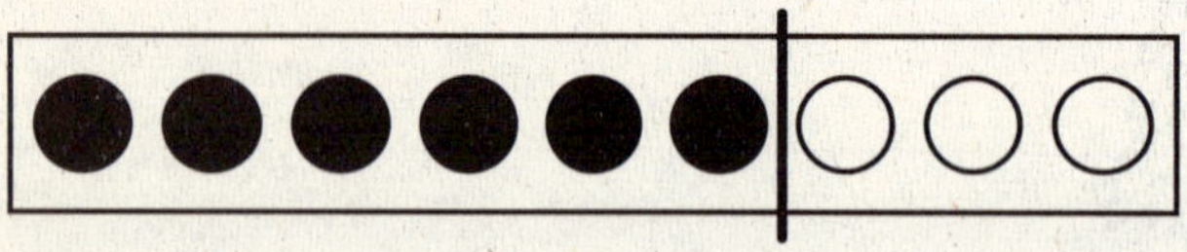

- ○ 5 + 4 and 4 + 5
- ○ 3 + 4 and 4 + 3
- ● 6 + 3 and 3 + 6
- ○ 1 + 8 and 8 + 1

14. Which shows the 8-partners and the switched partners?

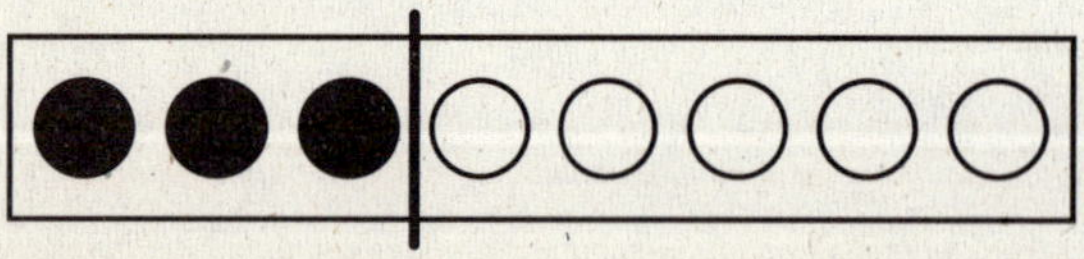

- ○ 3 + 4 and 4 + 3
- ● 3 + 5 and 5 + 3
- ○ 2 + 6 and 6 + 2
- ○ 2 + 5 and 5 + 2

15. Which shows the number 7?

○ 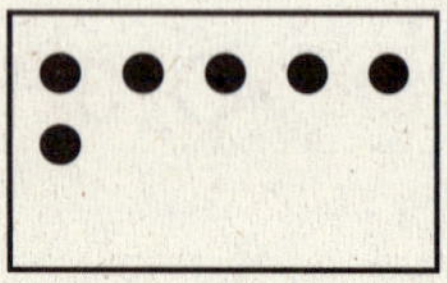 ● 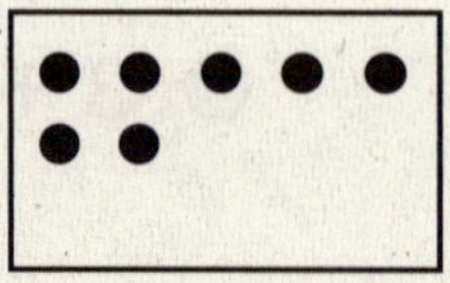 ○ 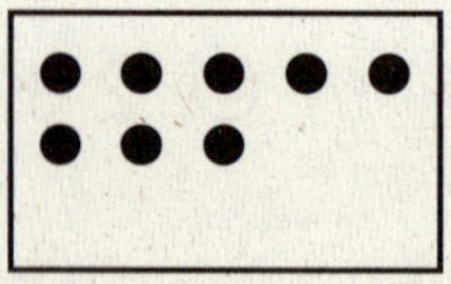 ○ 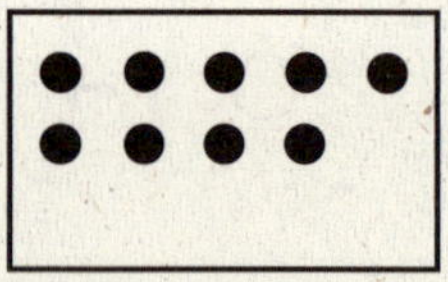

16. Which shows the number 6?

○ 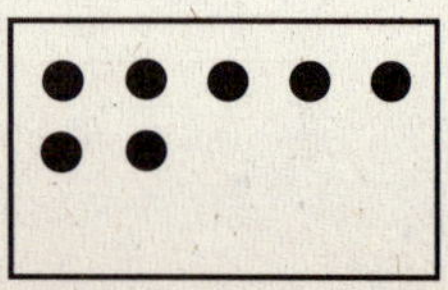 ● 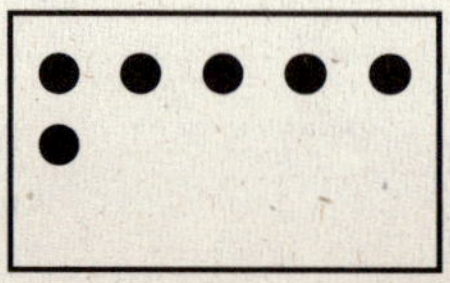 ○ 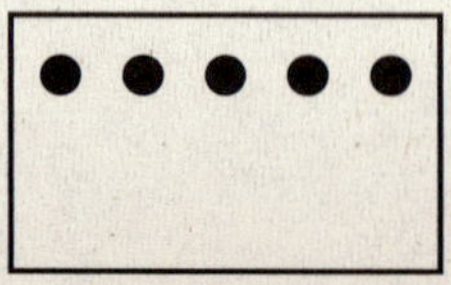 ○ 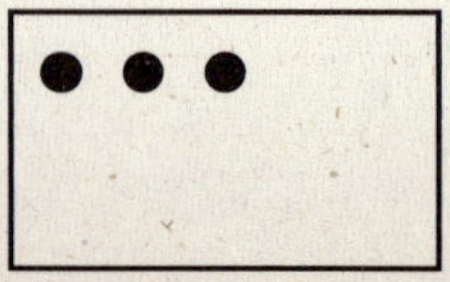

Name

17. Which shows the number 8?

○ 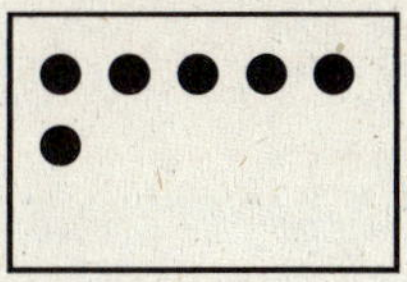
○ 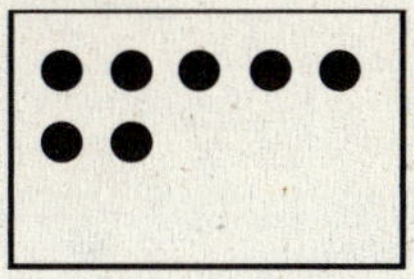
● 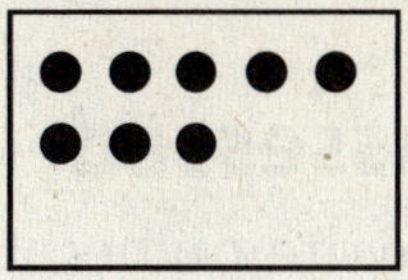
○ 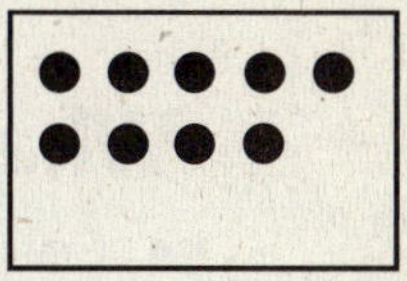

Is the number odd or even?

18. 

○ odd

● even

19. 

● odd

○ even

20. Which drawing shows 3 triangles?

○ 
● 
○ 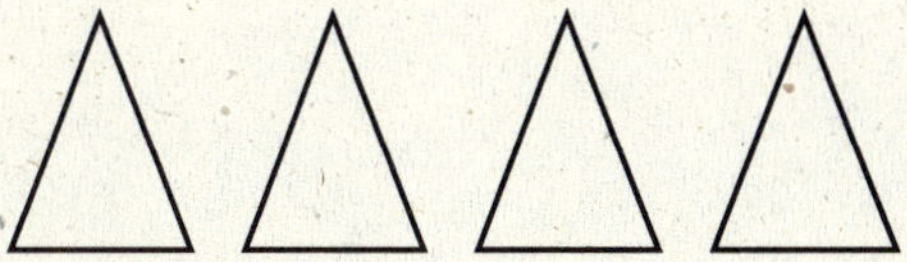
○ 

Early Number Activities

What Is Assessed

- Count and write numerals 1–10.
- Identify groups with up to 10 objects.
- Find the partners of numbers through 10.

Explaining the Assessment

1. Show the children several crayons. Ask a volunteer to choose four crayons from the group. Show the class the four and count them together. Point out the colors chosen.
2. Tell the children they will be choosing flowers for flowerpots.
3. Read the task aloud to the class. You may want to read one instruction at a time, then wait for children to complete it.

Materials

Crayons

Possible Responses

1. A drawing of 5 flowers in the pot. Some are yellow and some are red.
2. Children can write the partners of 5 that their drawings show, for example, 4 + 1 and 1 + 4.
3. A drawing of 7 flowers in the pot. Some are blue and some are yellow.
4. Children can write the partners of 7 that their drawings show, for example, 3 + 4 and 4 + 3.

Name

ACTIVITY Plant Flowers

1. Draw 5 flowers growing in the pot.
   Make some red. Make some yellow.

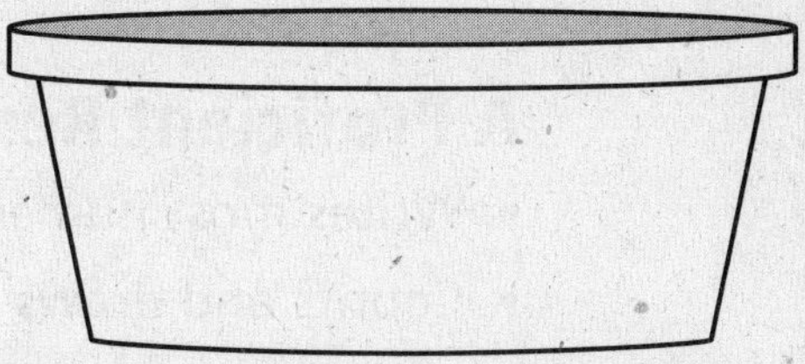

2. Write the partners of 5 the flowers show. Then switch the partners.

+		+

3. Draw 7 flowers growing in this pot.
   Make some blue. Make some yellow.

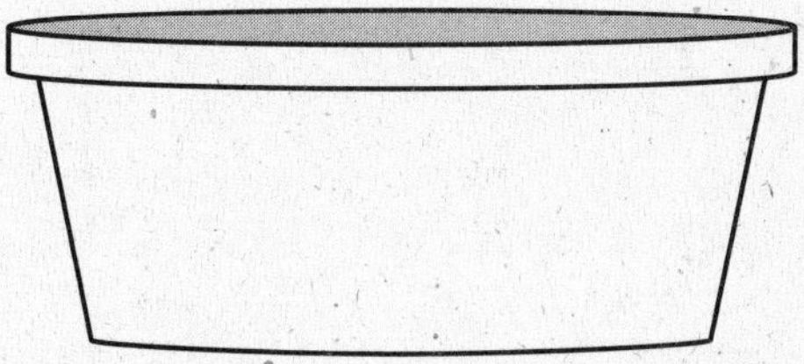

4. Write the partners of 7 the flowers show. Then switch the partners.

+		+

Performance Assessment Rubric

An Exemplary Response (4 points)

- Writes numerals correctly
- Counts and draws groups with 5 and 7 items correctly
- Identifies and writes correct partners of 5 and of 7

A Proficient Response (3 points)

- Writes most numerals correctly; may reverse a numeral
- Counts and draws groups with 5 and 7 items correctly
- Identifies and writes correct partners of 5 and/or of 7

An Acceptable Response (2 points)

- Writes some numerals correctly
- Counts or draws a group of 5 or 7 items correctly
- May make errors in identifying and writing partners of 5 and of 7

A Limited Response (1 point)

- May include many numerals that are not recognizable
- May not correctly count or draw a group of 5 or 7 items
- Includes many errors in identifying and writing partners of 5 and of 7

Unit 2
Quick Quiz 1

Name ______________________________

Write the partners and the total for each picture.

1. 5 + 1

Total 6

2. 2 + 5

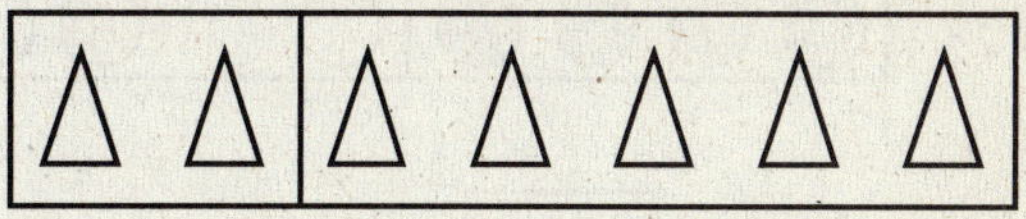

Total 7

3. 4 + 4

Total 8

4. 3 + 2

Total 5

Name ____________________

Write the partners and the total. Then write the equation.

1. 4 + 5

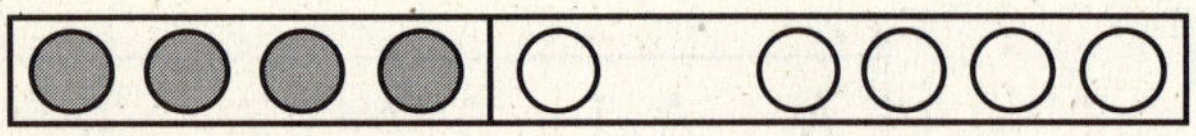

$4 + 5 = 9$

Equation

Total 9

2. 2 + 4

$2 + 4 = 6$

Equation

Total 6

Write how many cents in the group.

3.

7 ¢

Write the cost of the toys together.

4.

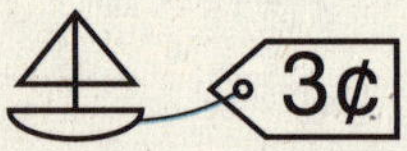

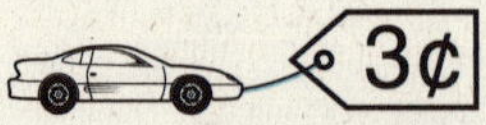

3 + 3 = 6 ¢

Name ______________________

Write how many are left. Use the picture to help you.

1. There were 9 apples.

$9 - 5 =$ 4

Then 5 were eaten.

2. There were 10 pencils.

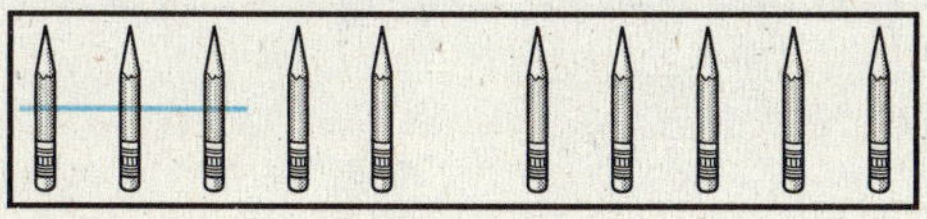

$10 - 3 =$ 7

Then 3 were lost.

3. There were 8 airplanes.

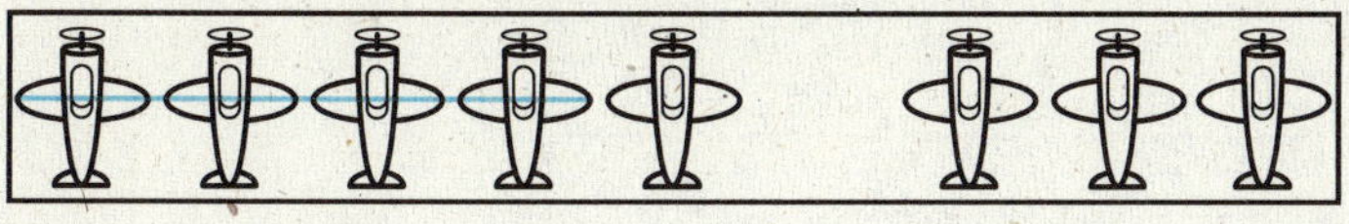

$8 - 4 =$ 4

Then 4 flew away.

Subtract and write the equation.

4. 

Subtract 6

$9 - 6 = 3$

Equation

5. 

Subtract 5

$7 - 5 = 2$

Equation

Name ____________________

Write the partners and the total for each picture.

1. [2] + [5]

Total [7]

2. [6] + [3]

Total [9]

3. [3] + [3]

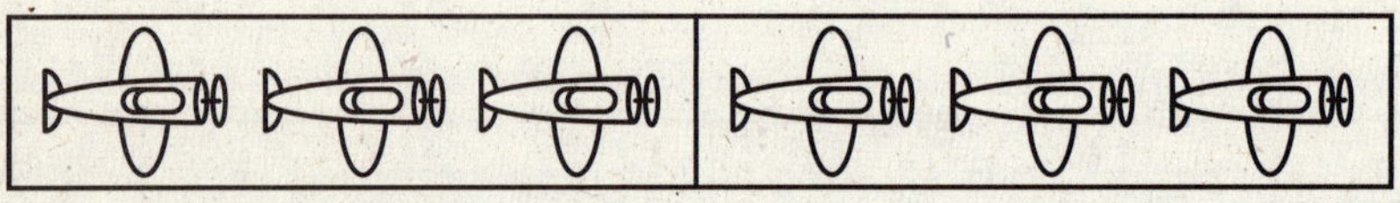

Total [6]

Write how many are left. Use the picture to help you.

4. There were 7 cars.

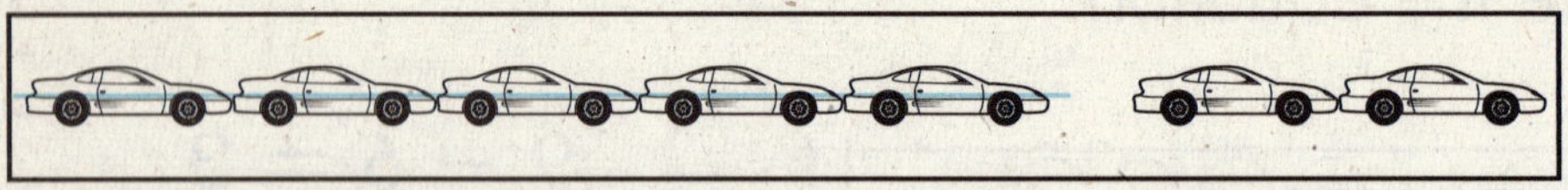

7 − 5 = [2]

Then 5 drove away.

5. There were 9 oranges.

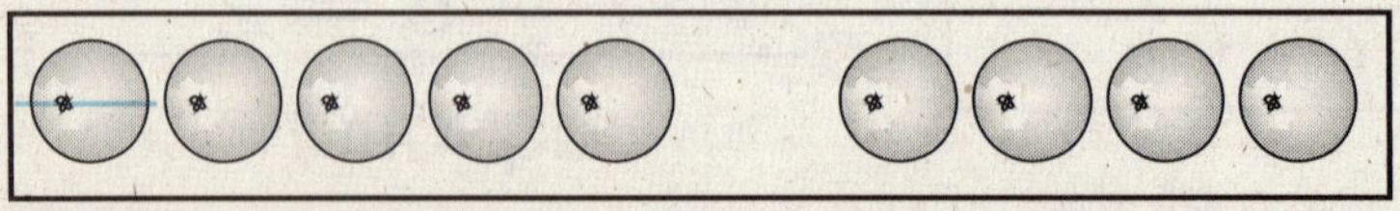

9 − 1 = [8]

Then 1 was eaten.

Name ______________________________

Write how many cents in each group.

1.  [8] ¢

2.  [10] ¢

Write the cost of the toys together.

3. 

[5] + [3] = [8] ¢

4. 

[2] + [4] = [6] ¢

Write the partners and the total for each picture.

5. [2] + [4]

Total [6]

6. [6] + [3]

Total [9]

7. [3] + [4]

Total [7]

8. [4] + [1]

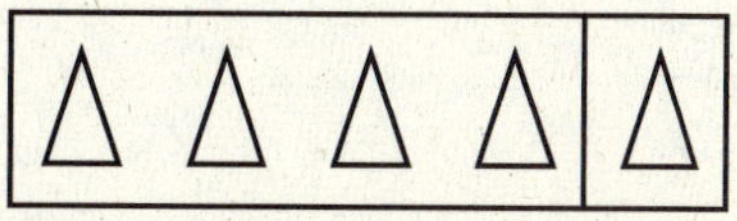

Total [5]

Name

Write the partners and total. Then write the equation.

9. 6 + 3

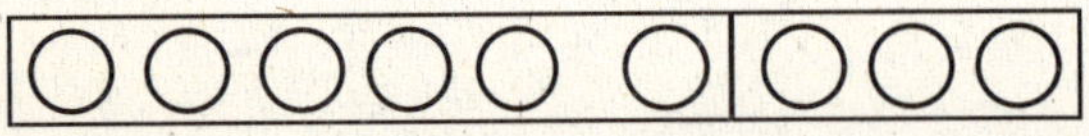

Total 9

6 + 3 = 9
Equation

10. 4 + 4

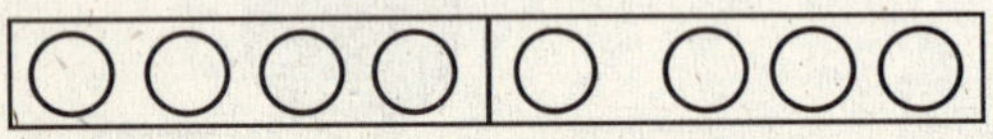

Total 8

4 + 4 = 8
Equation

Count on. Write the total.

11. 4  = Total 7

12. 3  = Total 9

Use the pictures. Subtract the numbers.

13.

$$\begin{array}{r} 9 \\ -\ 3 \\ \hline 6 \end{array}$$

14.

$$\begin{array}{r} 7 \\ -\ 5 \\ \hline 2 \end{array}$$

Name

Write how many are left. Use the picture to help you.

15. There were 10 buttons.

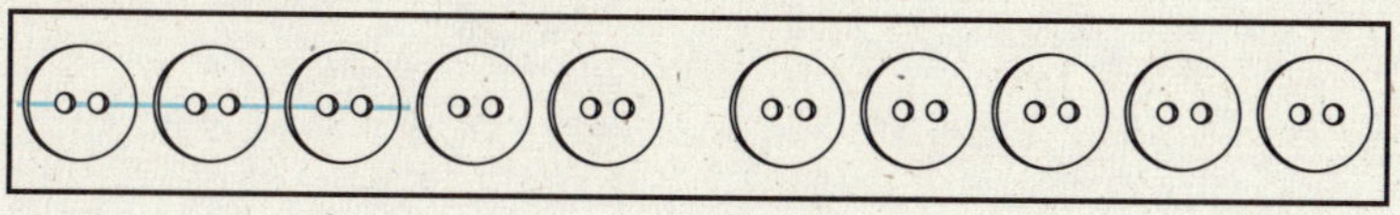

$10 - 3 =$ [7]

Then 3 fell off.

16. There were 9 hats.

$9 - 4 =$ [5]

Then 4 were sold.

Subtract and write the equation.

17.

Subtract 7

$9 - 7 = 2$

Equation

18.

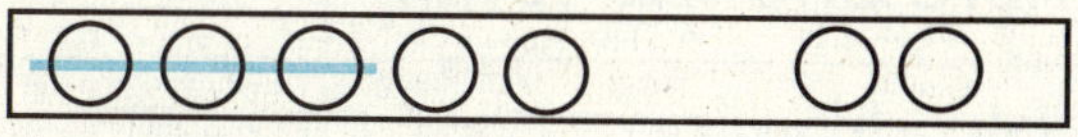

Subtract 3

$7 - 3 = 4$

Equation

19.

Subtract 5

$10 - 5 = 5$

Equation

Name

Add the numbers.

20. 7 + 1 = 8

21. 4 + 5 = 9

22. 4 + 4 = 8

Subtract the numbers.

23. 9 − 3 = 6

24. 5 − 2 = 3

25. **Extended Response** Draw squares to show 3 + 5. Then write an equation that shows the partners and the total.

Drawings will vary. Possible drawing □□□ □□□□□

3 + 5 = 8

Unit 2 Test **Form B**

Name ______________________________

Fill in the ○ for the correct answer.

How many cents are in each group?

1.

○ 6¢ ○ 7¢ ○ 8¢ ● 9¢

2.

○ 7¢ ● 6¢ ○ 5¢ ○ 4¢

What is the cost of the toys together?

3.

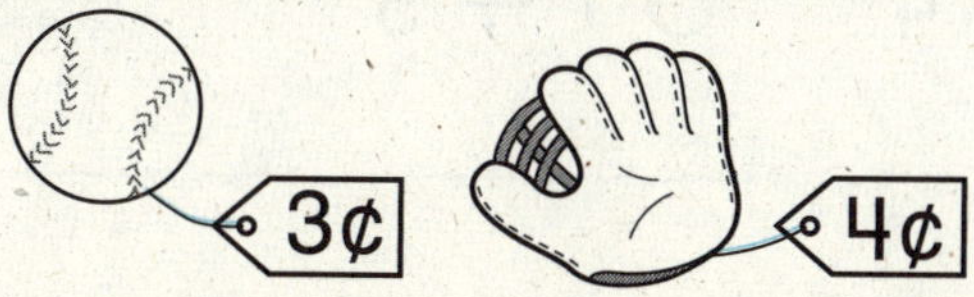

○ 5¢ ○ 6¢ ● 7¢ ○ 8¢

4.

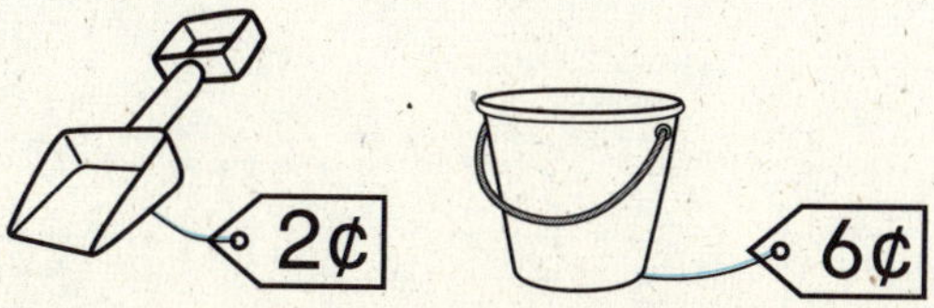

● 8¢ ○ 7¢ ○ 6¢ ○ 5¢

Name ______________________________

What are the partners for each picture?

5. ☐ + ☐

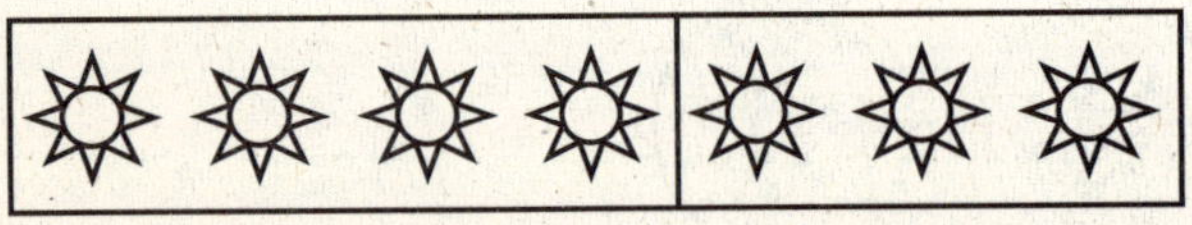

Total [7]

● 4 + 3 ○ 4 + 4 ○ 5 + 3 ○ 3 + 3

---

6. ☐ + ☐

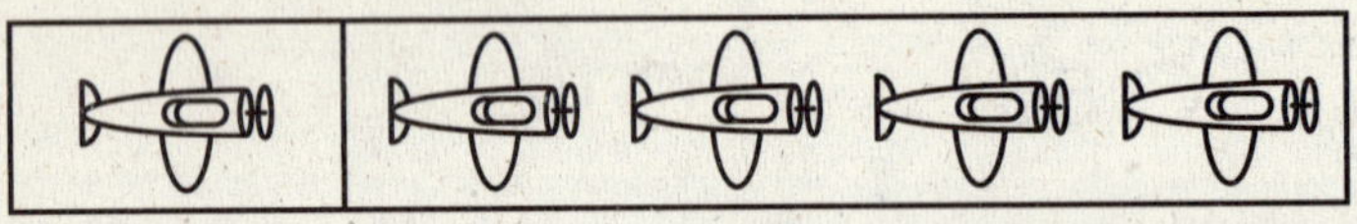

Total [5]

○ 2 + 2 ○ 2 + 4 ● 1 + 4 ○ 1 + 5

What is the total for the picture?

7. [5] + [3]

Total ☐

○ 5 ○ 6 ○ 7 ● 8

Name

What is the total for the picture?

8. 3 + 3

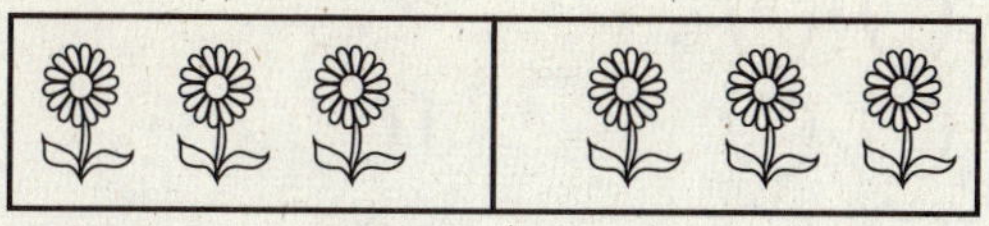

Total

○ 5 ● 6 ○ 7 ○ 8

What is the equation for each picture?

9.

○ 5 + 2 = 7 ○ 5 + 3 = 8

● 6 + 2 = 8 ○ 6 + 2 = 9

10.

● 5 + 1 = 6 ○ 5 + 1 = 5

○ 4 + 1 = 6 ○ 4 + 1 = 5

Count on. What is the total?

11.

= Total

○ 4 ○ 5

● 9 ○ 10

12.

= Total

○ 9 ● 8

○ 7 ○ 4

Name

Use the pictures. Subtract the numbers.

13.

$$\begin{array}{r} 7 \\ -\ 3 \\ \hline \end{array}$$

○ 7 ○ 6
○ 5 ● 4

14.

$$\begin{array}{r} 10 \\ -\ 2 \\ \hline \end{array}$$

● 8 ○ 7
○ 6 ○ 5

How many are left? Use the picture to help you.

15. There were 7 sailboats.

Then 4 sailed away.

○ 2 ● 3
○ 4 ○ 5

16. There were 10 pencils.

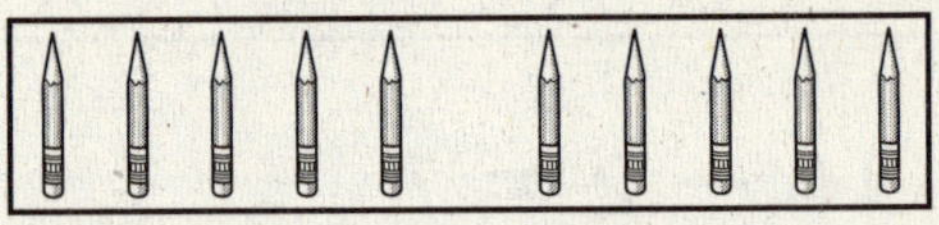

Then 4 were lost.

○ 3 ○ 4
○ 5 ● 6

What is the subtraction equation for each picture?

17.

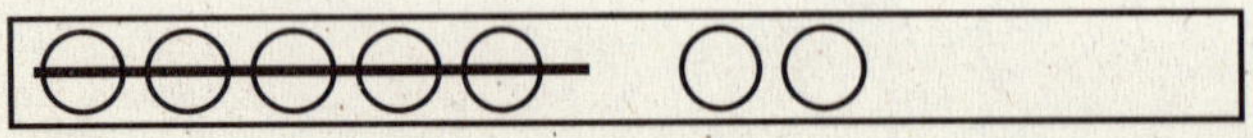

○ $7 - 6 = 1$ ● $7 - 5 = 2$
○ $5 - 3 = 2$ ○ $5 - 2 = 3$

18.

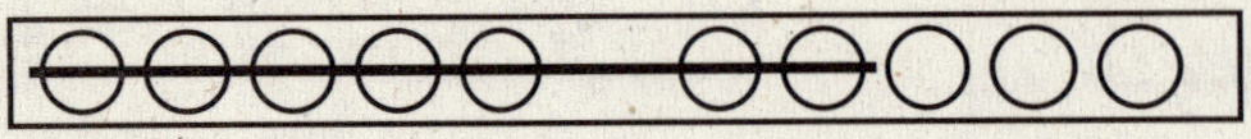

● $10 - 7 = 3$ ○ $10 - 7 = 2$
○ $7 - 4 = 3$ ○ $7 - 3 = 4$

Name

What is the subtraction equation for the picture?

19. 

○ 6 − 1 = 5 ○ 7 − 1 = 6

● 9 − 8 = 1 ○ 9 − 8 = 2

What is the total?

20. 3 + 6 = ☐ ○ 6 ○ 8 ● 9 ○ 10

21. 4 + 4 = ☐ ○ 4 ○ 7 ● 8 ○ 9

22. 5 + 3 = ☐ ○ 7 ● 8 ○ 9 ○ 10

What is the partner?

23. 8 − 6 = ☐

○ 6 ○ 4 ○ 3 ● 2

24. 9 − 3 = ☐

○ 4 ○ 5 ● 6 ○ 7

25. Which drawing shows 5 + 3?

○ 

● 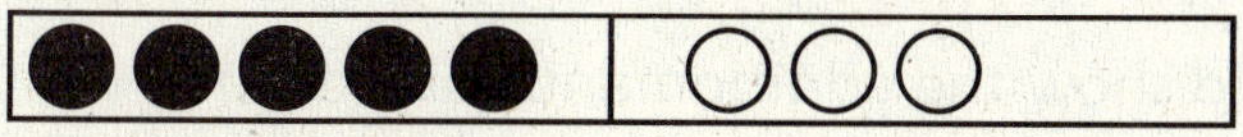

○ 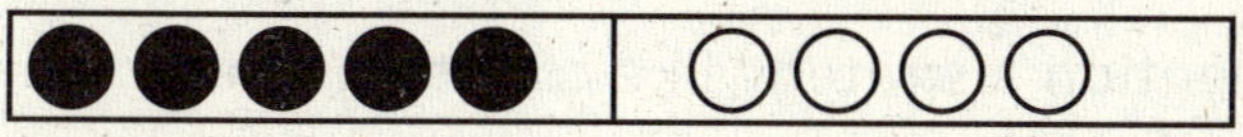

○ 

Unit 2

Operations and Simple Equations

What Is Assessed

- Represent and solve addition picture problems.
- Write and solve addition equations.
- Use the counting on strategy for finding the total.

Explaining the Assessment

1. Have a volunteer take a handful of red centimeter cubes and place them where the class can see them. Count them together.

2. Read the activity aloud to the class. You may want to read one instruction at a time, then wait for children to complete it.

Materials

Red and blue centimeter cubes (10 cubes total)

Possible Responses

Question 1: Answers will vary.

Question 2: Answers will vary.

Question 3: The equation should show the addition and total of the answers to Questions 1 and 2.

Question 4: Answers will vary.

Question 5: Answers will vary.

Question 6: The equation should show the addition and total of the answers to Questions 4 and 5.

Question 7: Answers will vary.

Question 8: The equation should show the addition and total of the cubes drawn in Question 7.

Question 9: Children should mention a strategy like counting one group, then counting on to find the total.

Name ______________________________

ACTIVITY How Many?

1. Take some red cubes in one hand.
   How many red cubes do you have? ____________

2. Take some blue cubes in the other hand.
   How many blue cubes do you have? ____________

3. Write an equation to show how many cubes you have in all.

   ________ + ________ = ________

Take a different number of red and blue cubes.

4. How many red cubes? ________

5. How many blue cubes? ________

6. Write an equation. ________ + ________ = ________

7. Take a different number of red and blue cubes.
   Draw how many red cubes and blue cubes you have.

8. Write an equation. ________ + ________ = ________

9. Tell how you added your cubes.

____

____

Performance Assessment Rubric

An Exemplary Response (4 points)

- Clearly represents addition in pictures and in numeral equations
- Solves addition correctly and explains clearly how the problem was solved
- Chooses and applies appropriate solution strategies including counting on

A Proficient Response (3 points)

- Clearly represents addition in pictures and in numeral equations
- Solves addition correctly
- Partially explains how the problem was solved
- Chooses and applies appropriate solution strategies

An Acceptable Response (2 points)

- Represents addition with few errors
- Solves addition with few errors
- May not explain how the problem was solved
- Chooses appropriate solution strategies

A Limited Response (1 point)

- Represents addition with several errors
- May make several errors in solutions to addition
- May not explain how the addition was solved
- May choose inappropriate solution strategies

Unit 3
Quick Quiz 1

Name

Find the unknown partner or total.

1. $4 + 2 = \boxed{6}$

2. $3 + 6 = \boxed{9}$

3. $7 + 1 = \boxed{8}$

4. $5 + \boxed{5} = 10$

5. $6 + \boxed{2} = 8$

Name ______________________________

Solve the story problems.

Show your work. Use drawings, numbers, or words.

1. Leo had 9 apples. Then he ate 4 of them. How many does he have now?

apple

[5] apples
label

2. There were 8 fish in a pond. Then 5 swam away. How many fish are left?

pond

[3] fish
label

3. Vanya had 6 pencils. Then she gave 4 away. How many pencils does she have now?

pencil

[2] pencils
label

Unit 3
Quick Quiz 3

Name

Find the unknown partner or total.

1. $4 + 5 = \boxed{9}$

2. $2 + \boxed{6} = 8$

Solve the story problems.

Show your work. Use drawings, numbers, or words.

3. Gina had 3 kittens. Then she got 4 more. How many kittens does she have now?

kitten

7 kittens
label

4. There were 6 ducks on the lake. Then 3 more came. How many ducks are there in all?

lake

9 ducks
label

5. Carlo had 5 flowers. Then his friend gave him 5 flowers. How many flowers does Carlo have now?

flower

10 flowers
label

Unit 3
Quick Quiz 4

Name

Find the unknown partner or total. Watch the signs.

1. 5 + 4 = [9]

2. 8 + [2] = 10

3. 6 + [1] = 7

4. 7 − 5 = [2]

5. 9 − 2 = [7]

6. 6 − 3 = [3]

Unit 3 Test
Form A

Name ______

Find the unknown partner or total. Watch the signs.

1. $3 + 4 = \boxed{7}$

2. $4 + 2 = \boxed{6}$

3. $7 + \boxed{3} = 10$

4. $5 + \boxed{4} = 9$

5. $9 - 2 = \boxed{7}$

6. $10 - 4 = \boxed{6}$

7. $7 - 5 = \boxed{2}$

8. $5 - 1 = \boxed{4}$

Solve the story problems.

Show your work. Use drawings, numbers, or words.

9. Edie had 4 crayons. Then she found 2 more. How many crayons does she have now?

You may read the problems to children if they are not ready to read independently.

6 crayons
label

10. There were 3 fish in a fishbowl. Then 5 more fish were put in. How many fish are there in all?

8 fish
label

Name

Solve the story problems.

Show your work. Use drawings, numbers, or words.

11. Luis saw 4 geese in the pond. He saw more on the shore. Altogether he saw 7 geese. How many were on the shore?

3 geese
label

12. There were 4 apples in a bowl. Then Rita put 3 more apples in the bowl. How many apples are there now?

7 apples
label

13. Miko had 1 nickel. Then she found 4 pennies in her pocket. How many cents does she have now?

9 ¢

14. Norm had 1 nickel and 2 pennies. He found 1 more penny on the table. How many cents does he have now?

8 ¢

Name

Solve the story problems.

Show your work. Use drawings, numbers, or words.

15. There were 8 cars. Then 5 drove away. How many were left?

car

3

cars
label

16. Mom made 5 pancakes. Dad made some too. Together they made 10 pancakes. How many pancakes did Dad make?

pancake

5

pancakes
label

17. There were 6 ducks at the park. Then 3 flew away. How many ducks are left?

park

3

ducks
label

18. Li had 9 cats. He gave 7 away. How many are left?

cat

2

cats
label

Name

Solve the story problems.

Show your work. Use drawings, numbers, or words.

19. Nadia had 1 nickel and 5 pennies. Then she spent 4 pennies on a pencil. How many cents does she have now?

6 ¢

20. **Extended Response** Write a story problem about pennies. Solve your story problem using pictures, numbers, or words.

Check children's work.

*Item 20 also assesses the Process Skills of Communication and Representation.

Name ______________________________

Fill in the ○ for the correct answer.

What is the unknown partner or total? Watch the signs.

1. $3 + 5 = \square$

○ 9 ● 8 ○ 7 ○ 6

2. $4 + 4 = \square$

○ 6 ○ 7 ● 8 ○ 9

3. $1 + \square = 9$

● 8 ○ 7 ○ 6 ○ 5

4. $6 + \square = 8$

○ 5 ○ 4 ○ 3 ● 2

5. $9 - 3 = \square$

○ 4 ○ 5 ● 6 ○ 7

6. $7 - 6 = \square$

● 1 ○ 2 ○ 3 ○ 4

Name

7. $10 - 7 = \square$

○ 6 ○ 5 ○ 4 ● 3

8. $8 - 2 = \square$

○ 7 ● 6 ○ 5 ○ 4

Solve the story problems.

Show your work. Use drawings, numbers, or words.

9. Frida had 4 pencils. Then she found 4 more. How many pencils does she have now?

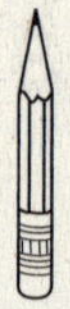
pencil

○ 6 pencils ○ 7 pencils

● 8 pencils ○ 9 pencils

10. There were 6 rabbits in the yard. Then 3 more rabbits came. How many rabbits are there in all?

rabbit

● 9 rabbits ○ 8 rabbits

○ 7 rabbits ○ 6 rabbits

Name

Solve the story problems.

Show your work. Use drawings, numbers, or words.

11. Chan saw 7 birds in the tree and some more on the ground. There are 10 birds in all. How many birds are on the ground?

- ○ 10 birds
- ○ 9 birds
- ○ 7 birds
- ● 3 birds

12. There were 2 turtles on a rock. Then 5 more turtles came. How many turtles are there now?

- ○ 6 turtles
- ● 7 turtles
- ○ 8 turtles
- ○ 9 turtles

13. Mona had 1 nickel. Then she found 2 pennies on the table. How many cents does she have now?

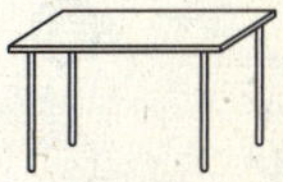

- ○ 8¢
- ● 7¢
- ○ 6¢
- ○ 5¢

Name

Solve the story problems.

Show your work. Use drawings, numbers, or words.

14. Pete had 1 nickel and 2 pennies. He found 1 more penny. How many cents does he have now?

nickel

○ 6¢ ○ 7¢

● 8¢ ○ 9¢

15. Bo had 8 caps. He gave 5 away. How many are left?

cap

○ 1 cap ○ 2 caps

● 3 caps ○ 4 caps

16. Liz picked 3 flowers. Teri picked some more. Together they picked 8 flowers. How many did Teri pick?

flower

○ 8 flowers ● 5 flowers

○ 4 flowers ○ 3 flowers

17. There were 7 ants on a rock. Then 2 crawled away. How many ants are left?

ant

○ 2 ants ○ 3 ants

○ 4 ants ● 5 ants

Name

Solve the story problems.

Show your work. Use drawings, numbers, or words.

18. Willie had 9 buttons. Then he gave 6 away. How many buttons does he have now?

button

○ 2 buttons ● 3 buttons
○ 4 buttons ○ 5 buttons

19. Oscar had 1 nickel and 3 pennies. Then he spent 4 pennies. How many cents does he have now?

nickel

○ 5¢ ● 4¢
○ 3¢ ○ 2¢

20. Which story problem has the answer "7 cents"?

○ There were 2 nickels in Jake's pocket. Then he put some pennies in his pocket. How many cents are in his pocket now?

○ Jake had 7 pennies. He found some more pennies and a nickel. How many nickels does Jake have now?

○ Jake had a nickel and some pennies in his pocket. He gave his sister 7 cents. Now he has 3 cents. How many pennies did Jake have?

● Jake had a nickel and some pennies in his pocket. He gave his sister 1 penny. Now he has 6 cents. How many cents did he have in his pocket?

Story Problem Strategies

What Is Assessed

- Represent and solve addition story problems.
- Solve addition equations.
- Represent and solve subtraction story problems.
- Solve subtraction equations.

Explaining the Assessment

1. Show 10 counters, a bowl, and Number Cards 1–9. Ask a child to choose a Number Card. Count out that many counters and place them under the bowl. Ask:

   - How many counters are there altogether?
   - How many counters are hiding?
   - How many counters are left?

   Repeat with other numbers.

2. Read the activity aloud with the class. In Questions 1 and 2, emphasize that children can choose any number at the top of the page, but that they need to choose different numbers for each problem.

Materials

10 counters, bowl, Number Cards 1–9

Possible Responses

Questions 1 and 2: Answers will vary depending on which numbers the children choose. Solutions may include drawings, counting on, Math Mountains, or equations.

Sample solutions:

4	●●●●●

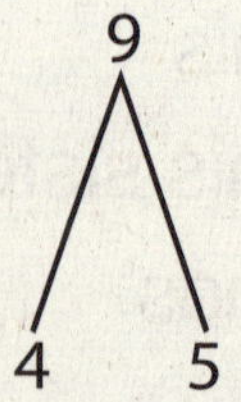

Question 3: Answers will vary.

Name

ACTIVITY Hide and Seek

Some children are playing hide and seek.
Choose one of these numbers for each ◯.

3 4 5 7

Solve the story problems.

1. 10 children are playing. ◯ go and hide. How many are left? ☐ ______ label	
2. ◯ children are hiding. ◯ more children hide. How many children are hiding? ☐ ______ label	

3. Write the equations for Problems 1 and 2.

______ ______

Performance Assessment Rubric

An Exemplary Response (4 points)

- Uses a mathematical strategy to solve each problem efficiently
- Solves addition and subtraction story problems correctly
- Writes addition and subtraction as an equation and solves both correctly

A Proficient Response (3 points)

- Uses a mathematical strategy to solve each problem
- Solves addition or subtraction story problem correctly
- Writes addition and subtraction as an equation but solves one incorrectly

An Acceptable Response (2 points)

- Shows a strategy to solve each problem
- Solves addition or subtraction story problems correctly
- Writes addition or subtraction equation incorrectly

A Limited Response (1 point)

- Shows random or unidentifiable strategies to solve each problem
- Solves addition or subtraction story problems correctly
- Writes incomplete addition or subtraction equations

Name ____________________

Write the number.

1.  36

2.  62

Draw 10-sticks and circles.

3. 27 

4. 45 

Solve the story problems.

Show your work. Use drawings, numbers, or words.

5. There are 6 pens in a box and 6 extra pens. How many in all?

12 pens
label

6. There are 9 apples on the tree. There are 6 apples on the ground. How many apples in all?

15 apples
label

Unit 4
Quick Quiz 2

Name ______________________

1. How many stars?

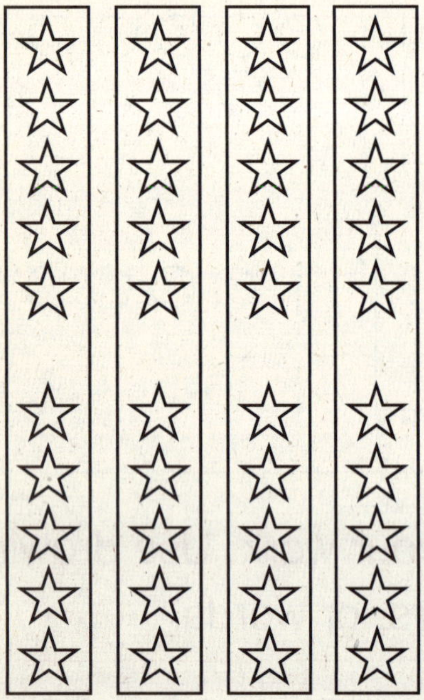

40

2. How many balls?

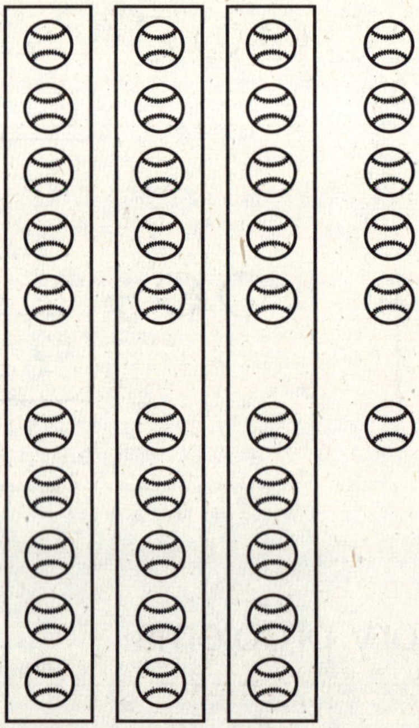

36

Find the total.

3. 8 + 5 = 13

4. 12 + 7 = 19

Write the word name.

5. 7 = seven

Unit 4
Quick Quiz 3

Name ________________________________

Find the total.

1. 15 + 7 = 22

2. 23 + 8 = 31

3. 14 + 5 = 19

Write the word name.

4. 19 = nineteen

5. 90 = ninety

Name ______________________

Write the number.

1. 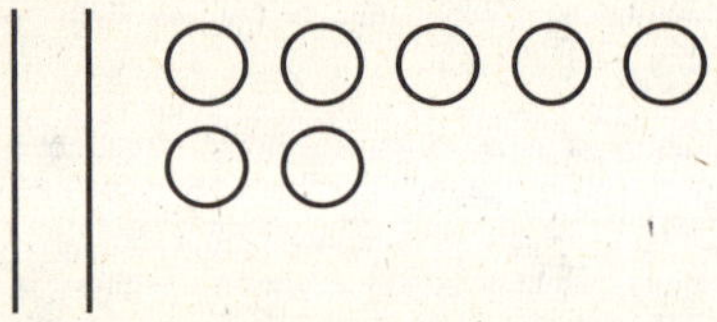

27

2. 

51

Draw 10-sticks and circles.

3. 34

4. 67

5. How many apples?

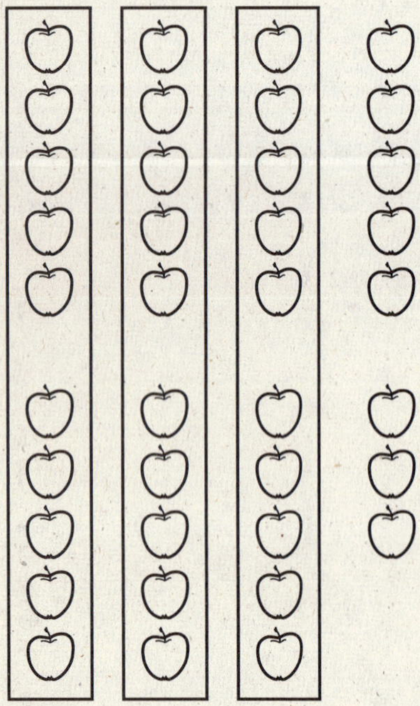

38

6. How many bananas?

12

Name

How many muffins?

7. 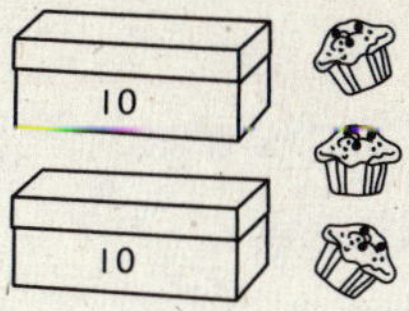

23

8. 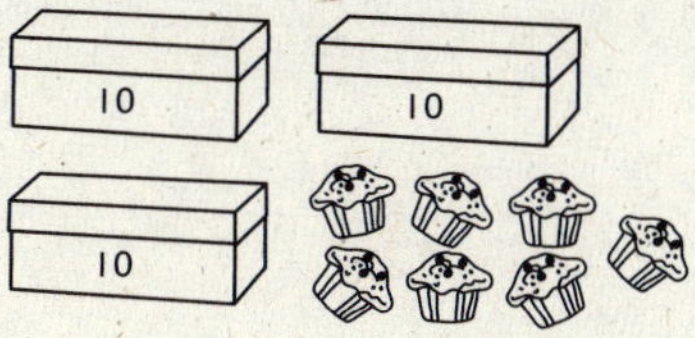

37

9. 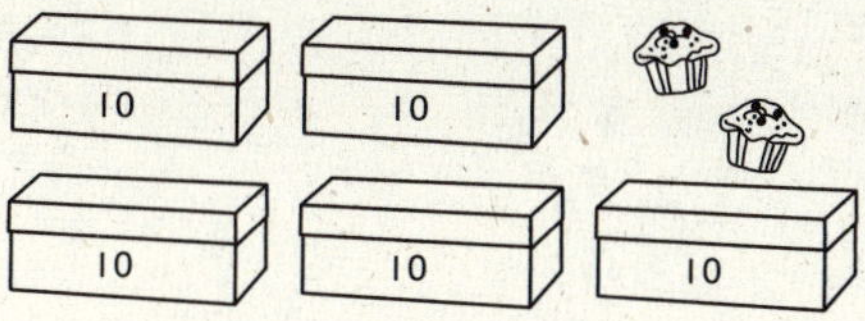

52

Find the total. Then write the word name for the total.

10. 10 + 5 = 15

fifteen

11. 24 + 2 = 26

twenty-six

12. 45 + 7 = 52

fifty-two

13. 39 + 4 = 43

forty-three

14. 26 + 7 = 33

thirty-three

Name

Solve the story problems.

Show your work. Use drawings, numbers, or words.

15. There are 8 oranges in a box and 3 extra oranges. How many are there in all?

orange

11	oranges
	label

16. Jess has a box of 12 crayons and 6 extra crayons. How many crayons does she have?

crayon

18	crayons
	label

17. There were 4 bees. Then 7 more bees came. How many bees are there now?

bee

11	bees
	label

18. There were 8 birds on the roof. Then 5 more came. How many birds are there now?

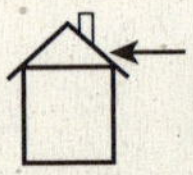
roof

13	birds
	label

Name

Complete the exercises.

19. 30 + 5 = 35

20. 3 + 5 = 8

21. 30 + 50 = 80

22. 80 + 1 = 81

23. 8 + 1 = 9

24. 80 + 10 = 90

25. **Extended Response** Write a number greater than 10. Then draw 10-sticks and circles to show it.
Children's answers and drawings will vary.

Name ______________________________

Fill in the ○ for the correct answer.

What is the number?

1. 

○ 13 ● 25 ○ 27 ○ 52

2. 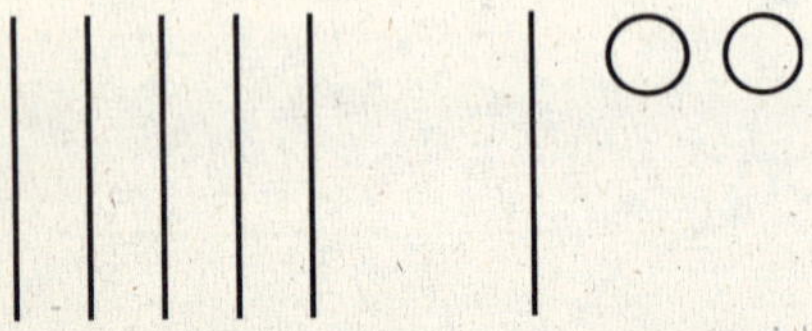

○ 16 ○ 46 ● 62 ○ 64

Which drawing shows the number?

3. 27

4. 64

Name

5. How many leaves?

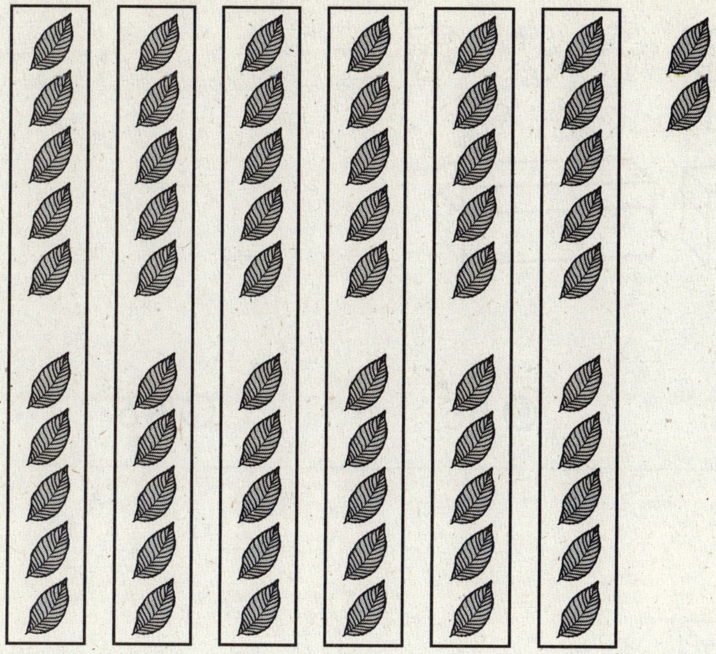

○ 51 ● 62 ○ 68 ○ 72

6. How many baseballs?

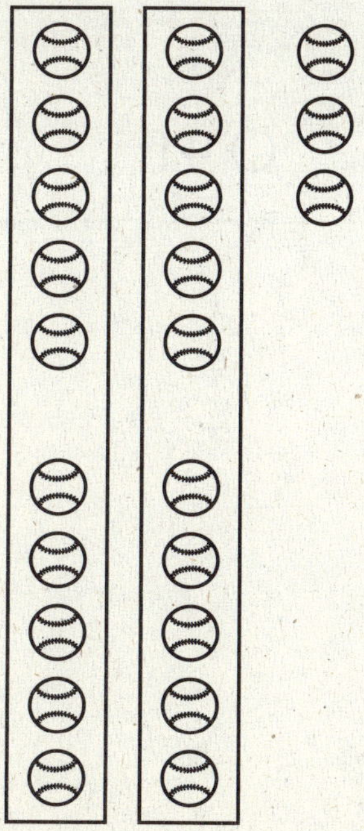

● 23 ○ 26 ○ 31 ○ 33

7. How many muffins?

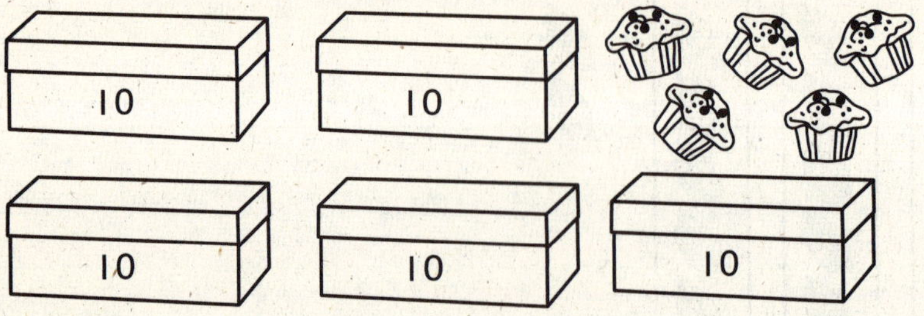

○ 67 ○ 58 ● 55 ○ 46

8. How many muffins?

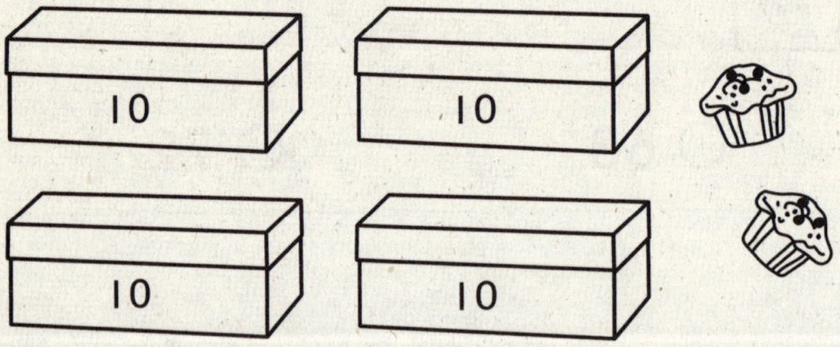

○ 61 ○ 52 ● 42 ○ 41

9. How many muffins?

○ 38 ● 36 ○ 28 ○ 26

Name ______________________________

Find the total.

10. 30 + 5 = ☐

- ○ 25
- ○ 30
- ● 35
- ○ 40

11. 26 + 2 = ☐

- ○ 24
- ● 28
- ○ 36
- ○ 46

12. 12 + 9 = ☐

- ○ 12
- ○ 19
- ○ 20
- ● 21

13. 28 + 4 = ☐

- ● thirty-two
- ○ thirty
- ○ twenty-eight
- ○ twenty-four

14. 57 + 8 = ☐

- ○ sixty-eight
- ○ sixty-six
- ● sixty-five
- ○ fifty-nine

Name

Solve the story problems.

15. There are 12 eggs in a carton and 3 extra eggs. How many eggs are there in all?

- ○ 9 eggs
- ○ 12 eggs
- ○ 14 eggs
- ● 15 eggs

16. Emily has a bag of 10 marbles and 6 extra marbles. How many marbles does she have?

- ○ 18 marbles
- ● 16 marbles
- ○ 14 marbles
- ○ 12 marbles

17. There were 8 squirrels. Then 4 more came. How many squirrels are there now?

- ○ 8 squirrels
- ○ 10 squirrels
- ● 12 squirrels
- ○ 14 squirrels

18. There were 5 dogs in the park. Then 6 more came. How many dogs are there now?

- ○ 16 dogs
- ○ 15 dogs
- ○ 13 dogs
- ● 11 dogs

Name

Complete the exercises.

19. $20 + 3 = \square$

○ 203 ○ 32 ● 23 ○ 20

20. $2 + 3 = \square$

● 5 ○ 6 ○ 23 ○ 32

21. $20 + 30 = \square$

○ 23 ○ 32 ● 50 ○ 230

22. $40 + 3 = \square$

○ 34 ● 43 ○ 304 ○ 403

23. $4 + 3 = \square$

○ 43 ○ 34 ● 7 ○ 6

24. $40 + 30 = \square$

○ 430 ○ 403 ● 70 ○ 60

25. Look at the 10-sticks and circles.
What number is shown?

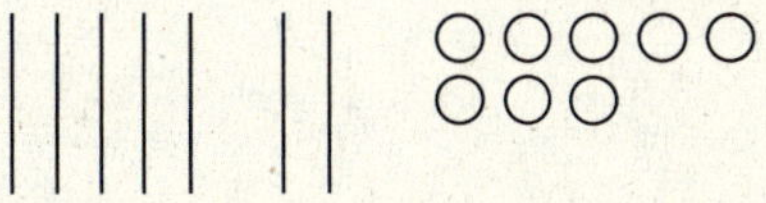

○ 89 ○ 88 ○ 79 ● 78

Unit 4

Basic Ten-Structured Concepts

What Is Assessed

- Represent 2-digit numbers.
- Add two 1-digit numbers.
- Solve problems with 2-digit numbers.

Explaining the Assessment

1. Read the activity aloud to the class. Read one instruction at a time, then wait for children to complete it.

Possible Responses

Question 1: Children should ring one kind of milk and show the number with 10-sticks and circles.

Question 2: Yes; answers will vary but should include adding 9 + 7 to find 16.

Question 3: Children should show numbers of two or more kinds of drinks that total 26. Numbers of each kind of drink should not exceed what is available. Children may use 10-sticks and circles or another method to show their work.

Name ______________________________

ACTIVITY Snack Time

It is snack time. The class has these drinks.

Milk		Juice	
Chocolate Milk	White Milk	Orange Juice	Apple Juice
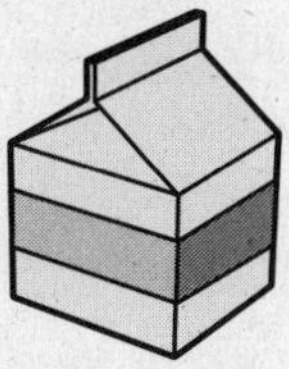		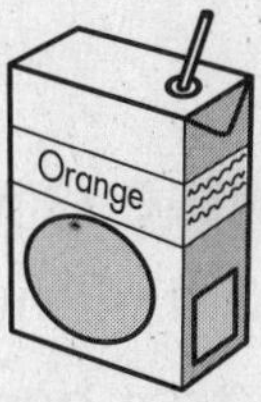	
23 cartons	17 cartons	9 boxes	7 boxes

1. Ring one kind of milk. Draw 10-sticks and circles to show the number.

2. Are there enough juice boxes for 16 children? ____________

How do you know? Write or draw your answer.

3. There are 26 children in the class. Each chooses one drink. Show one way the children could choose drinks.

Drink	How many?

Performance Assessment Rubric

An Exemplary Response (4 points)

- Accurately and clearly represents 2-digit numbers with 10-sticks and circles
- Includes a justification that demonstrates understanding of 1-digit addition and an appropriate solution method
- Uses an efficient strategy to correctly solve problems with 2-digit numbers

A Proficient Response (3 points)

- Accurately represents 2-digit numbers with 10-sticks and circles
- Includes a justification that demonstrates understanding of 1-digit addition and an appropriate solution method
- Uses an efficient strategy to solve problems with 2-digit numbers; may make a calculation error

An Acceptable Response (2 points)

- Represents 2-digit numbers with 10-sticks and circles with few errors
- Includes a justification that demonstrates some understanding of 1-digit addition and an appropriate solution method
- Solves problems with 2-digit numbers with any strategy; may make a calculation error

A Limited Response (1 point)

- Makes several errors in representing 2-digit numbers with 10-sticks and circles
- Includes a justification that demonstrates little understanding of 1-digit addition or an appropriate solution method
- May choose an inappropriate strategy to solve problems with 2-digit numbers

Unit 5
Quick Quiz 1

Name ______________________________

How many cents?

10 10 10 1 1 1 1 1

1.  35 ¢

2.  24 ¢

3.  51 ¢

4.  42 ¢

5.  16 ¢

Name ______________________

Add the numbers.

1. 51 + 40 = [91]

2. 16 + 50 = [66]

Find the unknown 100-partners.

3. 30 + [70] = 100

4. 60 + [40] = 100

Continue the pattern.

5.

24 34 44 54 64 74 84

Name _______________ Date _______________

Solve the story problems.

Show your work. Use drawings, numbers, or words.

1. Today, Reina rode her bike for 4 miles in the morning and 3 miles in the afternoon. How far did she ride today?

bike

[7] miles
label

2. Jane picked 15 berries. Then she ate 8 of them. How many berries are left?

berries

[7] berries
label

Complete the exercises. Watch the signs.

3. $4 + 9 =$ [13]

4. $10 - 7 =$ [3]

5. $12 - 7 =$ [5]

6. $3 + 8 =$ [11]

Name ____________________

How many cents?

10 10 10 10 10 1 1

1.  52 ¢

2.  43 ¢

3.  34 ¢

Continue the pattern.

4. 13 23 33 43 53 63 73 83

5. 27 37 47 57 67 77 87 97

6. 16 26 36 46 56 66 76 86

7. 11 21 31 41 51 61 71 81

Name

Solve the story problems.

Show your work. Use drawings, numbers, or words.

8. Adam picked 16 berries. Then he ate 7 of them. How many berries are left?

9	berries
	label

9. Isa has 9 crayons and I have 8. How many crayons do we have in all?

17	crayons
	label

10. We saw 12 turtles at the pond. 7 of them were brown. How many of them were not brown?

5	turtles
	label

11. Today, Dana rode her bike for 8 miles in the morning and 6 miles in the afternoon. How far did she ride today?

14	miles
	label

Name

Add the numbers.

12. 47 + 20 = 67

13. 23 + 50 = 73

14. 29 + 40 = 69

15. 14 + 60 = 74

Find the unknown 100-partner.

16. 80 + 20 = 100

17. 30 + 70 = 100

18. 60 + 40 = 100

19. 10 + 90 = 100

Complete the exercises. Watch the signs.

20. 7 + 8 = 15

21. 14 − 6 = 8

22. 19 − 9 = 10

23. 6 + 7 = 13

24. Draw the fewest coins for 43¢.

Possible answer:

(10) (10) (10) (10) (1) (1) (1)

25. **Extended Response** Suppose you have 44 cents. You have no nickels. What coins could you have? Write or draw your answer.

Answers will vary. Possible answer:

(10) (10) (10) (10) (1) (1) (1) (1)

*Item 25 also assesses the Process Skills of Reasoning and Representation.

Name ______________________________

Fill in the ○ for the correct answer.

How many cents?

10 10 10 10 10 1 1

1. 

○ 35¢ ○ 43¢ ● 52¢ ○ 55¢

2. 

○ 15¢ ● 25¢ ○ 34¢ ○ 52¢

3. 

○ 51¢ ○ 44¢ ● 42¢ ○ 24¢

Name

Which continues the pattern?

4. 15, 25, 35

● 45, 55, 65, 75, 85
○ 46, 56, 66, 76, 86
● 55, 65, 75, 85, 95
○ 56, 66, 76, 86, 96

5. 25, 35, 45

○ 35, 45, 55, 65, 75
○ 45, 55, 65, 75, 85
○ 54, 64, 74, 84, 94
● 55, 65, 75, 85, 95

6. 18, 28, 38

○ 37, 47, 57, 67, 77
○ 38, 48, 58, 68, 78
● 48, 58, 68, 78, 88
○ 49, 59, 69, 79, 89

7. 24, 34, 44

○ 44, 54, 64, 74, 84
○ 45, 55, 65, 75, 85
● 54, 64, 74, 84, 94
○ 55, 65, 75, 85, 95

Name

Solve the story problems.

Show your work. Use drawings, numbers, or words.

8. There were 16 children at the park. Then 9 of them went home. How many children are there now?

park

○ 16 children ○ 9 children
○ 8 children ● 7 children

9. Su Li picked up 5 books from the library. Jon picked up 6 books from the library. How many books did they pick up in all?

book

○ 16 children ○ 6 books
● 11 books ○ 13 books

10. Braedon and Carl saw 13 cars. 5 of them were blue. How many cars were not blue?

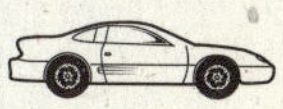

car

○ 13 cars ○ 9 cars
● 8 cars ○ 5 cars

11. Today, Darci picked 6 flowers this morning and 8 flowers this afternoon. How many flowers did she pick today?

flower

○ 2 flowers ○ 8 flowers
○ 13 flowers ● 14 flowers

Name

Add the numbers.

12. $37 + 40 = \square$

- ○ 57
- ○ 67
- ● 77
- ○ 87

13. $56 + 20 = \square$

- ○ 66
- ○ 70
- ● 76
- ○ 86

14. $13 + 30 = \square$

- ○ 16
- ○ 33
- ○ 36
- ● 43

15. $28 + 70 = \square$

- ○ 38
- ○ 58
- ○ 88
- ● 98

Name

Find the unknown 100 partner.

16. $60 + \square = 100$

- ○ 30
- ● 40
- ○ 30
- ○ 60

17. $50 + \square = 100$

- ○ 40
- ● 50
- ○ 60
- ○ 70

18. $20 + \square = 100$

- ○ 60
- ○ 70
- ● 80
- ○ 90

19. $90 + \square = 100$

- ○ 11
- ● 10
- ○ 1
- ○ 0

Add or subtract. Watch the signs.

20. $7 + 9 = \square$

- ○ 2
- ○ 15
- ● 16
- ○ 18

21. $11 - 3 \square =$

- ○ 5
- ● 8
- ○ 10
- ○ 14

22. $15 - 9 = \square$

- ○ 4
- ● 6
- ○ 7
- ○ 10

23. $6 + 7 = \square$

- ○ 1
- ○ 4
- ● 13
- ○ 15

Name

24. You have dimes, nickels, and pennies. Which shows the fewest coins for 36¢?

● 

○ 

○ 

○ 

25. Suppose you have 53 cents. You have no nickels. Which shows the coins you could have?

○ 

○ 

● 

○ 

Ten-Structured Applications

What Is Assessed

- Represent an amount less than one dollar with dimes and pennies.
- Add a decade number to any 2-digit number.
- Find the hundred partner of a decade number.
- Use ten-structure to identify a greater money amount.

Explaining the Assessment

1. Show the children pennies and dimes. Review how many cents each coin is worth. Ask children how many pennies could be fairly traded for one dime.
2. Read the task aloud with the class. You may wish to read one instruction at a time and wait for children to complete it.

Materials

Real or play money (pennies and dimes)

Possible Responses

Question 1: Child draws 3 dimes and 2 pennies, 2 dimes and 12 pennies, or 1 dime and 22 pennies.

Question 2: 52¢, check children's work.

Question 3: 40¢, explanations and drawings may vary.

Question 4: Child rings the group of coins with a value of 62¢. Explanations may vary, but should mention that there are more tens in 62 than there are in 26.

Name ____________________

ACTIVITY Dimes and Pennies

Dan saves his money in a jar.
He has 32 pennies.

1. Draw 32¢ with dimes and pennies.

2. Dan adds 20¢ to the jar. How many cents does he have in all? ____________
Show your work.

3. Dan saves more money. Now he has 60¢. How many more cents does he need to have 1 dollar? Draw or write how you know.

4. Which is more? Ring the coins. How did you decide?

____

Performance Assessment Rubric

An Exemplary Response (4 points)

- Correctly draws groups of dimes and pennies of a given value
- Adds a decade number to a 2-digit number correctly; clearly shows the addition
- Identifies the hundred partner of a decade number correctly
- Uses at least two of mathematical language, symbols, and diagrams to explain thoroughly
- Correctly compares values of groups of coins

A Proficient Response (3 points)

- Correctly draws groups of dimes and pennies of a given value
- Adds a decade number to a 2-digit number correctly; shows at least part of the addition
- Identifies the hundred partner of a decade number correctly
- Uses at least one of mathematical language, symbols, or diagrams to explain

An Acceptable Response (2 points)

- Draws groups of dimes and pennies of a given value nearly correctly
- Adds a decade number to a 2-digit number correctly; may not show work
- Identifies the hundred partner of a decade number correctly
- May include limited mathematical reasoning

A Limited Response (1 point)

- Makes many errors in drawing groups of dimes and pennies of a given value
- May add a decade number to a 2-digit number correctly; may not show work
- May not identify the hundred partner of a decade number correctly
- May include little or no explanation for answers

Unit 6 Quick Quiz 1

Name ____________________

Favorite Baseball Items

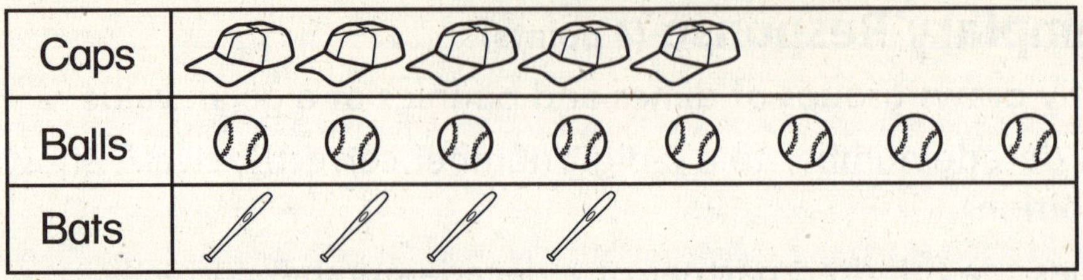

Use the graph to answer the questions below.

1. How many fewer caps are there than balls? 3

2. How many more balls are there than bats? 4

3. How many fewer bats are there than caps? 1

---

4. Make a picture graph about the shapes.

5. Complete the sentences. Ring the word **more** or **fewer**.

There are [2] (**more**) **fewer** triangles than stars.

There are [2] **more** (**fewer**) stars than triangles.

Unit 6
Quick Quiz 2

Name ______________________________

Solve the story problems.

1. Sara made 7 baskets. Jon made 4 more baskets than Sara. How many baskets did Jon make?

[11] baskets
label

2. Vera has 10 oranges. Rico has 2 fewer oranges than Vera. How many oranges does Rico have?

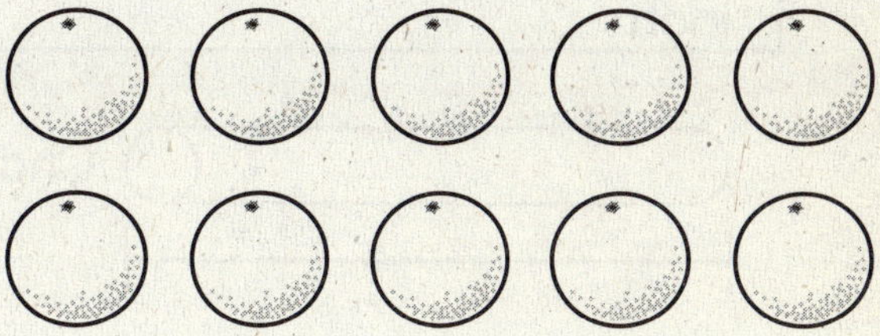

[8] oranges
label

3. Make a table from the picture graph below.

Picture Graph

Butterflies	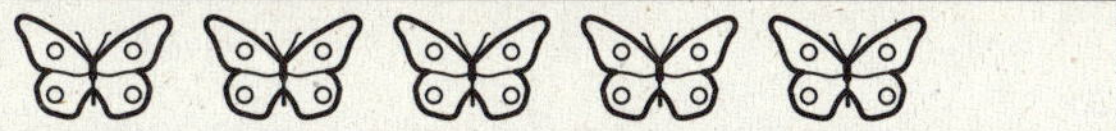
Ants	
Ladybugs	

Table

Insects	Number
Butterflies	5
Ants	6
Ladybugs	4

4. How many fewer butterflies are there than ants? 1

5. Are there more ladybugs or ants? ants

Unit 6
Quick Quiz 3

Name ______________________________

1. Measure the art supplies. Make a table of lengths.

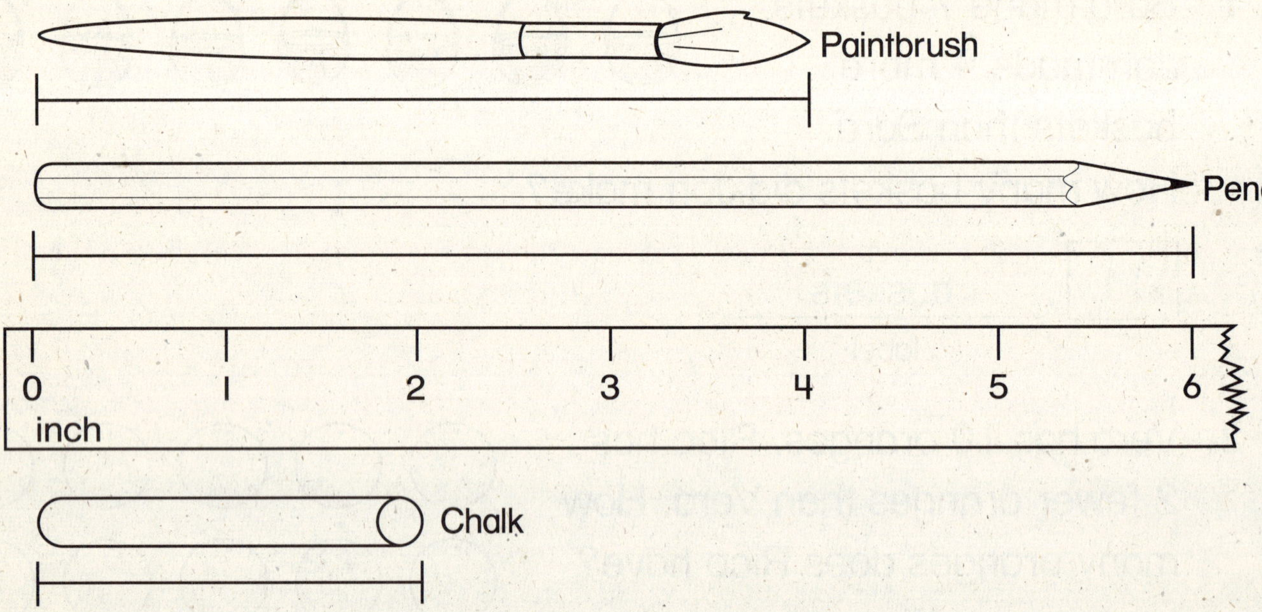

Object	**Length**
Paintbrush	4 inches
Pencil	6 inches
Chalk	2 inches

2. How much **shorter** is the paintbrush than the pencil?

2 inches

3. How much **longer** is the pencil than the chalk?

4 inches

4. How much **shorter** is the chalk than the paintbrush?

2 inches

Name ______________________

Fruit at the Market

Use the graph to answer the questions below.

1. Are there more apples or bananas? apples

2. Are there fewer bananas or oranges? bananas

3. The store has the most of which fruit? oranges

---

4. Make a picture graph about the shapes.

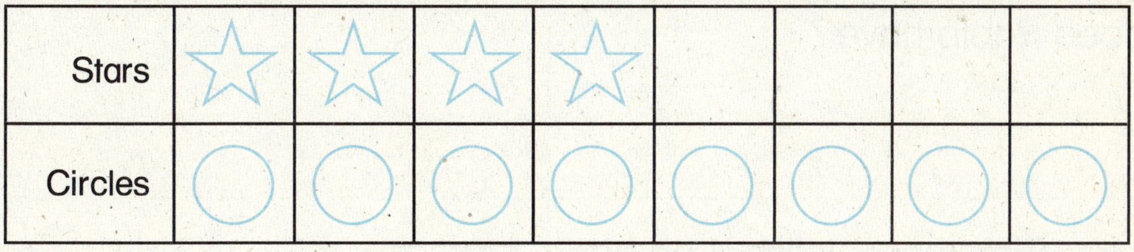

5. Complete the sentences. Ring the word **more** or **fewer**.

There are [4] **more** (circled) **fewer** circles than stars.

There are [4] **more** **fewer** (circled) stars than circles.

Name

Solve the story problems. Use drawings and numbers.

6. Jerry made 7 drawings. Ana made 6 more drawings than Jerry. How many drawings did Ana make?	6 drawings (label)
7. Mina has 9 apples. Peter has 7 apples. How many fewer apples does Peter have than Mina?	6 fewer apples (label)
8. Wendy has 7 stickers. Pablo has 3 fewer stickers than Wendy. How many stickers does Pablo have?	6 stickers (label)
9. Mrs. Sims has 11 fish. Lee has 6 fish. How many more fish does Mrs. Sims have than Lee?	6 more fish (label)

Name

Solve the story problems. Use drawings and numbers.

10. There were 16 birds. Now there are 6 fewer birds. How many birds are there?

10 birds
label

11. Elena has 12 marbles. Joe has 7 marbles. How many more marbles does Elena have than Joe?

5 more marbles
label

12. Make a table from this picture graph.

Picture Graph

Table

Animals	Number
Cats	3
Dogs	5
Rabbits	4

13. How many cats are there? 3 cats

14. Are there more rabbits or dogs? dogs

15. Are there fewer rabbits or cats? cats

Name ______________________________

16. Measure each vegetable. Complete the table.

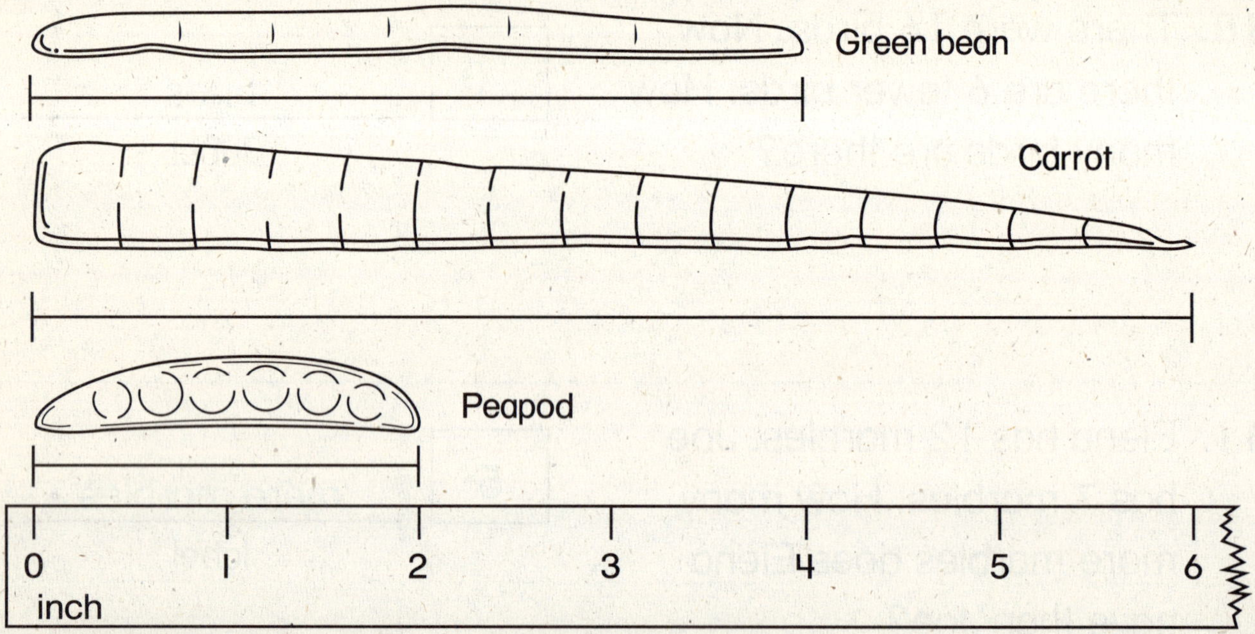

Vegetable	Length
Green bean	4 inches
Carrot	6 inches
Peapod	2 inches

17. How much shorter is the green bean than the carrot? __2__ inches

18. How much longer is the carrot than the peapod? __4__ inches

19. How much shorter is the peapod than the green bean? __2__ inches

20. **Extended Response** Write and answer a question to compare length.

Name ____________________

Fill in the ○ for the correct answer.

Balls for Gym Class

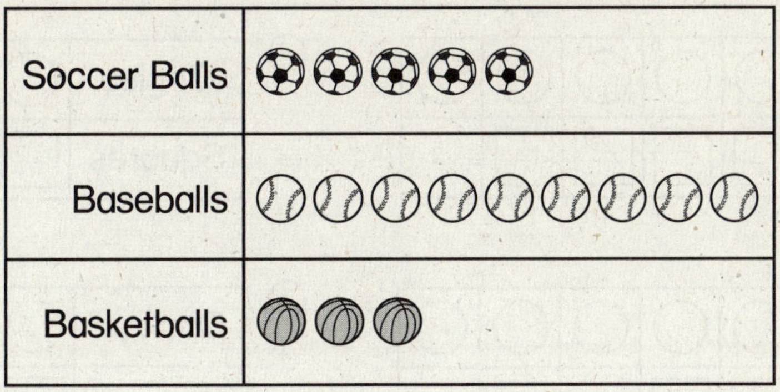

Use the graph to answer the questions below.

1. How many more soccer balls are there than basketballs?

● 2 ○ 3 ○ 4 ○ 5

2. How many fewer basketballs are there than baseballs?

○ 7 ● 6 ○ 5 ○ 3

3. The gym class has the most of which ball?

● Baseballs

○ Soccer balls

○ Basketballs

○ Soccer balls and basketballs

Name

4. Which picture graph is about the shapes?

○ 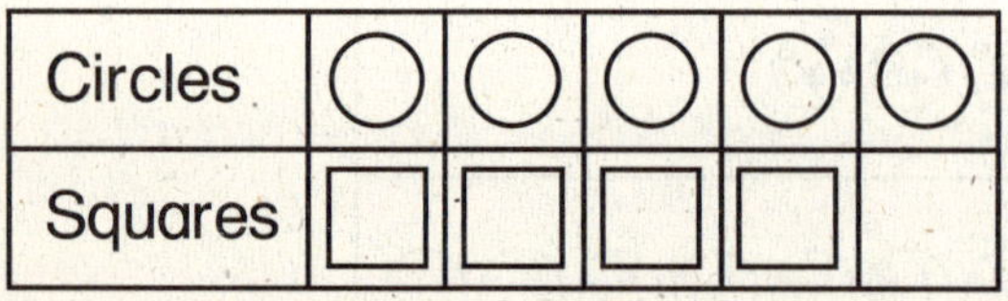

○ 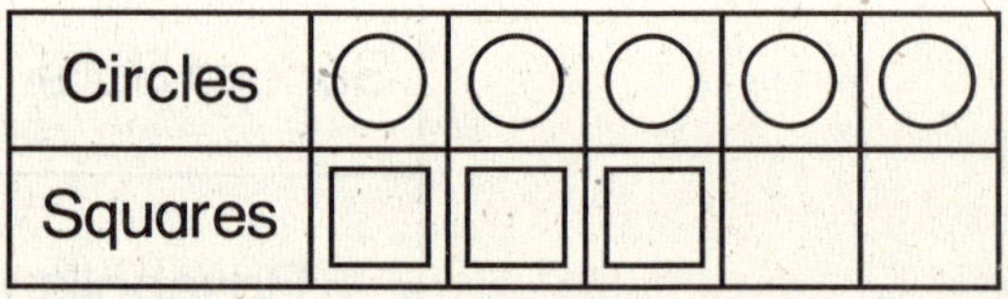

● 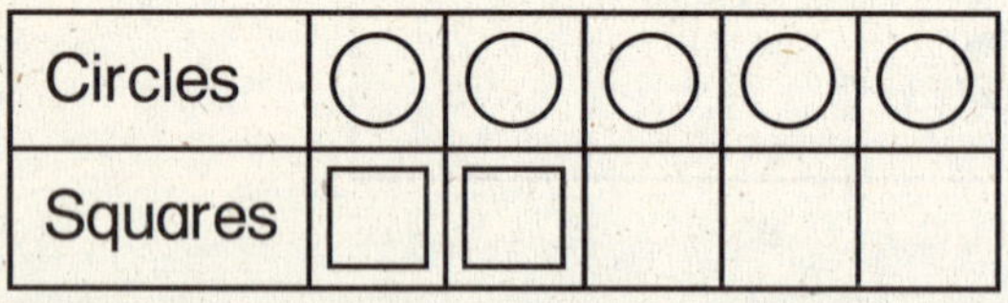

○ 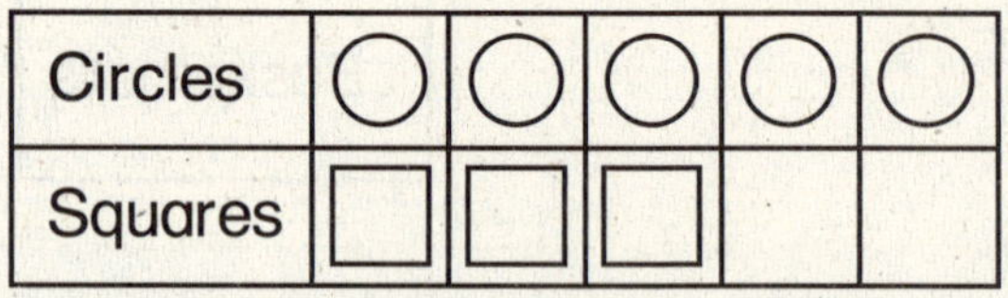

5. There are ______ more circles than squares.

○ 2 ● 3 ○ 4 ○ 5

Solve the story problems. Use drawings and numbers.

6. Mark has 6 berries. Velma has 8 more than Mark. How many berries does Velma have?

○ 10 berries ○ 13 berries
● 14 berries ○ 20 berries

7. Kaylee has 10 apples. Zoe has 3 apples. How many fewer apples does Zoe have than Kaylee?

○ 6 fewer apples ● 7 fewer apples
○ 12 fewer apples ○ 13 fewer apples

Name

Solve the story problems. Use drawings and numbers.

8. Raul has 13 cards. Ned has 5 fewer cards than Raul. How many cards does Ned have?

○ 6 cards ● 8 cards
○ 17 cards ○ 18 cards

9. Paul has 10 flowers. Ann has 8 flowers. How many more flowers does Paul have than Ann?

○ 18 more flowers ○ 12 more flowers
○ 4 more flowers ● 2 more flowers

10. There were 13 muffins this morning. There are 6 fewer this afternoon. How many muffins are there?

○ 19 muffins ○ 12 muffins
● 7 muffins ○ 6 muffins

11. Don has 8 crayons. Jake has 4 crayons. How many more crayons does Don have than Jake?

● 4 more crayons ○ 8 more crayons
○ 10 more crayons ○ 12 more crayons

Name

Use the graph to answer the questions below.

Picture Graph

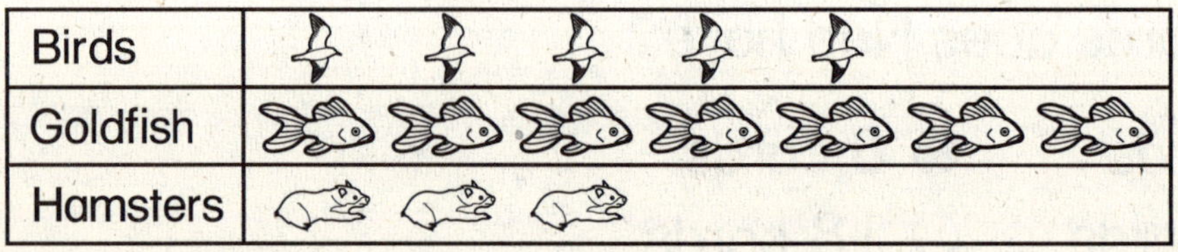

12. Which table shows the picture graph?

○

Animals	Number
Birds	3
Goldfish	7
Hamsters	5

●

Animals	Number
Birds	5
Goldfish	7
Hamsters	3

○

Animals	Number
Birds	7
Goldfish	5
Hamsters	3

○

Animals	Number
Birds	5
Goldfish	3
Hamsters	7

13. How many goldfish are there?

○ 3 ○ 5 ○ 6 ● 7

14. How many birds are there?

○ 3 ● 5 ○ 7 ○ 8

15. How many hamsters are there?

○ 7 ○ 4 ● 3 ○ 2

Name ____________________

Measure the toys. Use your measurements to answer the questions.

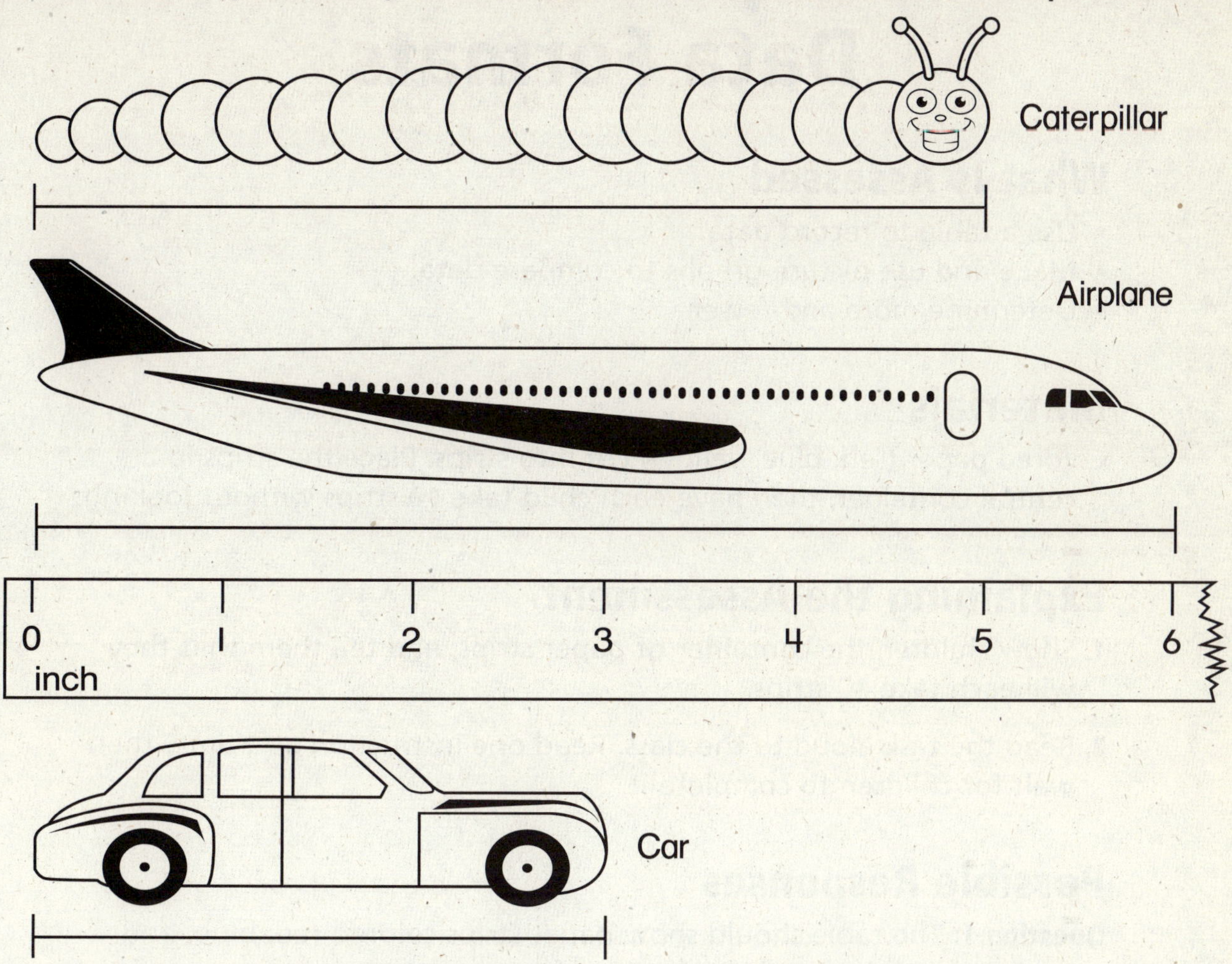

16. How long is the airplane?

○ 4 inches ○ 5 inches ● 6 inches ○ 8 inches

17. How long is the caterpillar?

○ 6 inches ● 5 inches ○ 4 inches ○ 2 inches

18. How long is the car?

○ 2 inches ● 3 inches ○ 4 inches ○ 5 inches

19. How much longer is the caterpillar than the car?

○ 1 inch ● 2 inches ○ 4 inches ○ 5 inches

20. How much shorter is the caterpillar than the airplane?

○ 4 inches ○ 3 inches ○ 2 inches ● 1 inch

Comparisons and Data Formats

What Is Assessed

- Use a table to record data.
- Make and use picture graphs to compare data.
- Determine *more* and *fewer.*

Materials

Colored paper (red, blue, yellow) cut into strips. Place the strips in a central container, then have each child take 10 strips without looking.

Explaining the Assessment

1. Show children the container of paper strips, and tell them that they will each take 10 strips.
2. Read the task aloud to the class. Read one instruction at a time, then wait for children to complete it.

Possible Responses

Question 1: The table should show paper strips colored red, blue, and yellow, and the number of strips of each color.

Question 2: Answers will vary, but should correspond to the table in Question 1.

Question 3: Answers will vary, but should correspond to the table in Question 1.

Question 4: The picture graph should show strips colored red, blue, and yellow, and dots representing the number of strips of each color. The picture graph should correspond to the table in Question 1.

Name

ACTIVITY Counting Colors

Take 10 colored strips.

1. Color each ▭ in the table below to match the word.
   Count how many strips of each color you have.
   Write the number in the table.

My Paper Strips

Color	Total
red	
blue	
yellow	

2. There are the most of which color? ______________

3. There are the fewest of which color? ______________

4. Make a picture graph to show the colors.

Colors										
▭										
▭										
▭										

Performance Assessment Rubric

An Exemplary Response (4 points)

- Accurately records colors and numbers of paper strips in a table
- Includes a clear, accurate, and well organized picture graph
- Identifies the color with the most strips and the color with the fewest strips

A Proficient Response (3 points)

- Accurately records colors and numbers of paper strips in a table
- Includes a clear picture graph with few or no errors
- Identifies the color with the most strips and the color with the fewest strips

An Acceptable Response (2 points)

- Records colors and numbers of paper strips in a table with few errors
- Includes a picture graph with few errors
- Identifies the color with the most strips or the color with the fewest strips

A Limited Response (1 point)

- May record colors or numbers in a table, possibly with many errors
- Includes a picture graph that may not reflect data in the table
- May identify the color with the most or the fewest strips

Unit 7
Quick Quiz 1

Name ______________________________

Ring half of the objects. Then fill in the blanks. Children can ring any half.

1. 

Half of __6__ is __3__.

2. 

Half of __10__ is __5__.

Add the numbers.

3. $6 + 6 =$ 12

4. $9 + 9 =$ 18

Solve the story problem.

Show your work. Use drawings, numbers, or words.

5. There are 7 squirrels on the ground. There are twice as many in the tree. How many squirrels are in the tree?

squirrel

14 __squirrels__
label

Unit 7
Quick Quiz 2

Name ______________________________

How much is shaded? Write $\frac{1}{2}$ or $\frac{1}{4}$.

1. 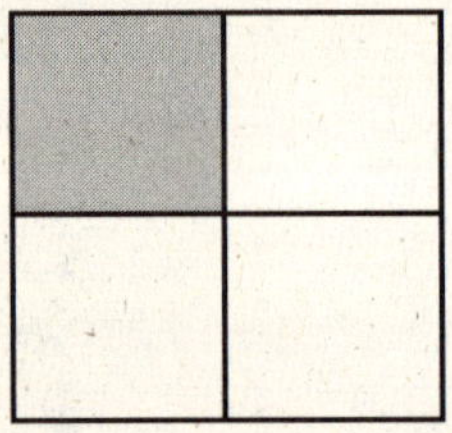

$\frac{1}{4}$

2. 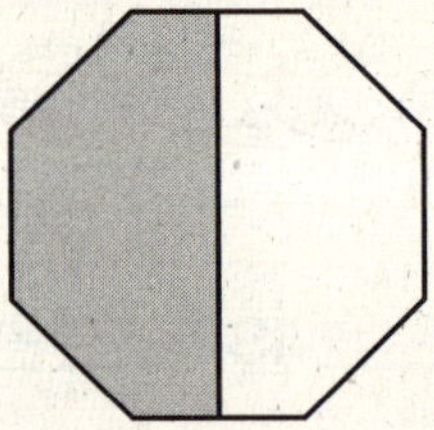

$\frac{1}{2}$

3. 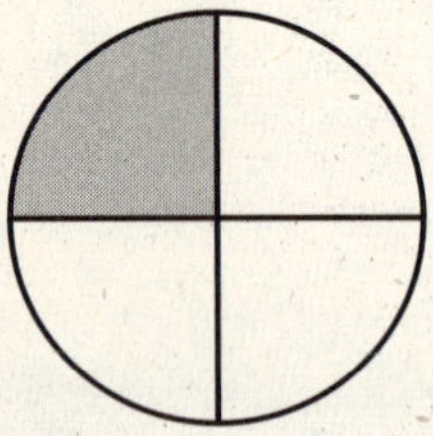

$\frac{1}{4}$

Ring one fourth of the objects. Then fill in the blanks. Children can ring any fourth.

4. 

One fourth of 8 is 2.

5. 

One fourth of 4 is 1.

6. 

One fourth of 12 is 3.

Unit 7
Quick Quiz 3

Name ____________________

Use the circle graph to answer the questions.

Animals at the Farm

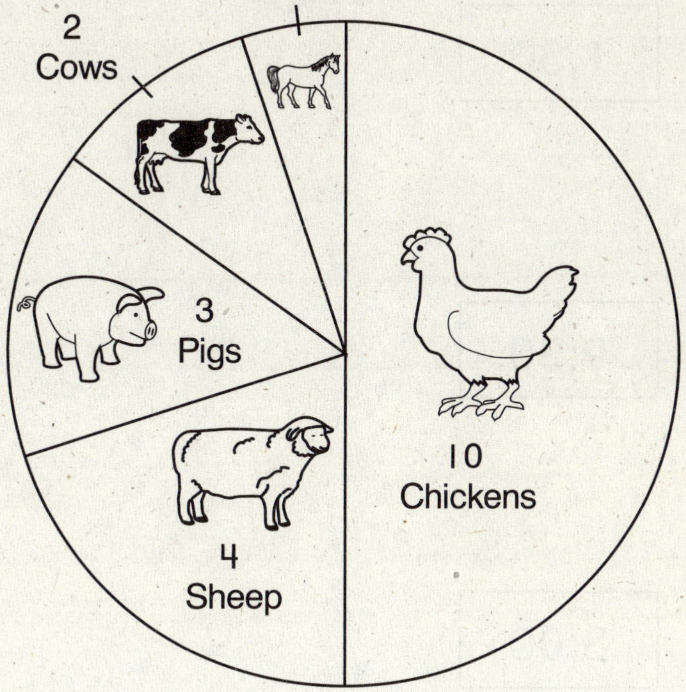

1. How many more sheep are there than cows? ___2___

2. How many fewer pigs are there than chickens? ___7___

3. The farm has the least of which animal? ___horse___

Unit 7
Quick Quiz 4

Name

Write the time.

1.

1:30

2.

9:30

3.

3:00

4. Draw hands on the clock to show the time.

7:00

5. Ring the month that comes before October.

November   September   August

Unit 7 Test
Form A

Name ______________________________

Use doubles to add.

1. $4 + 4 =$ 8

2. $9 + 9 =$ 18

3. $2 + 2 =$ 4

4. $5 + 5 =$ 10

Make each rectangle twice as big.

5.

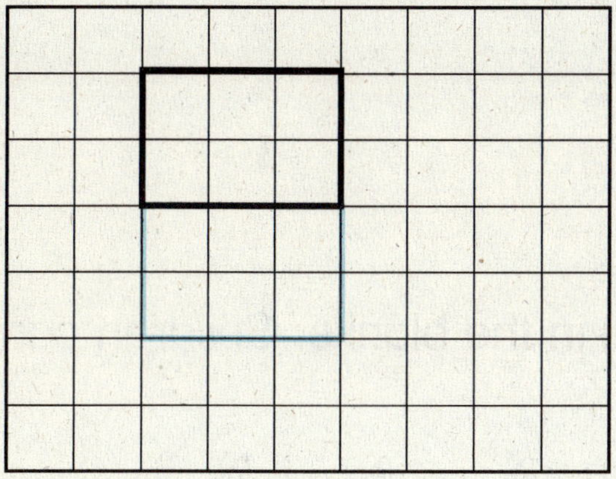

Possible drawing shown above.

6.

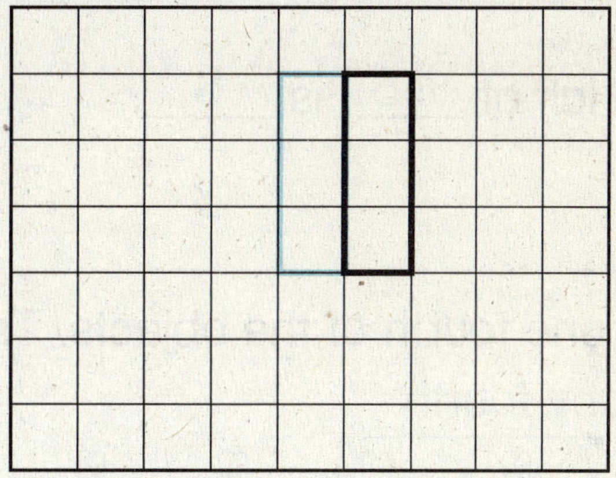

Possible drawing shown above.

How much is shaded? Write $\frac{1}{2}$ or $\frac{1}{4}$.

7.

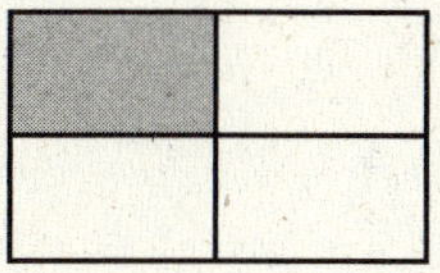

$\frac{1}{4}$

8.

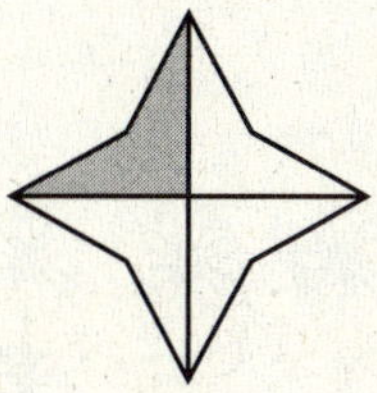

$\frac{1}{4}$

9.

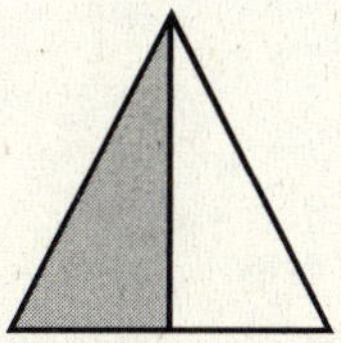

$\frac{1}{2}$

Name

Ring half of the objects. Then fill in the blanks. Children can ring any half.

10. 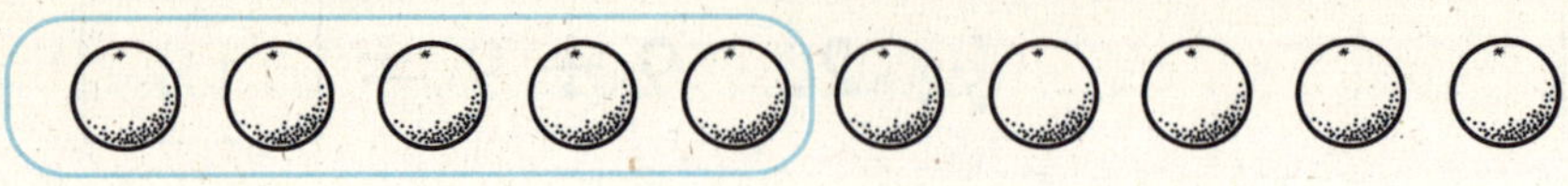

Half of __10__ is __5__.

11. 

Half of __16__ is __8__.

Ring one fourth of the objects. Then fill in the blanks. Children can ring any fourth.

12. 

One fourth of __8__ is __2__.

13. 

One fourth of __12__ is __3__.

Name

Use the circle graph to answer the questions.

Clothes at the Clothing Store

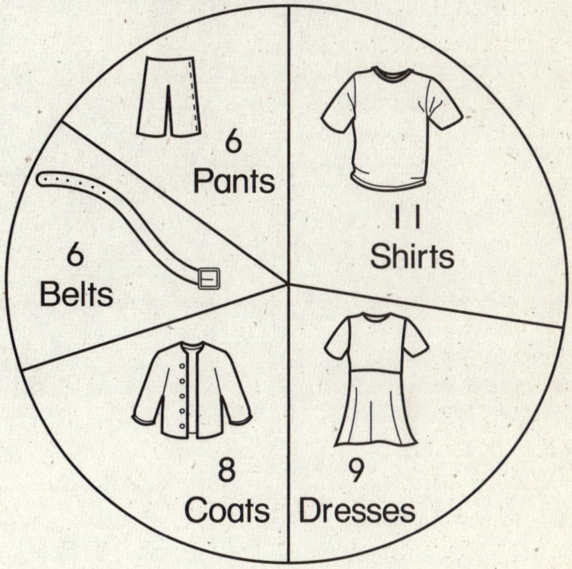

14. The clothing store has the most of which type of clothing?

Shirts

15. How many more dresses are there than pants?

3 dresses

16. How many fewer coats are there than shirts?

3 coats

Write the time in the boxes.

17.

6:00

18.

2:30

19. Ring the month that comes after April.

August

March

May

Name

20. Extended Response Write an equation with doubles and a teen total. Make a drawing of the doubles.

Sample answer: 8 + 8 = 16

*Item 20 also assesses the Process Skills of Connections and Representation.

Name ____________________

Fill in the ○ for the correct answer.

Use doubles to add.

1. 3 + 3 = ☐

○ 3 ○ 5 ● 6 ○ 7

2. 6 + 6 = ☐

○ 13 ● 12 ○ 11 ○ 10

3. 8 + 8 = ☐

○ 18 ○ 17 ● 16 ○ 15

4. 5 + 5 = ☐

○ 5 ○ 9 ● 10 ○ 11

How many more squares do you need to make each rectangle twice as big?

5.

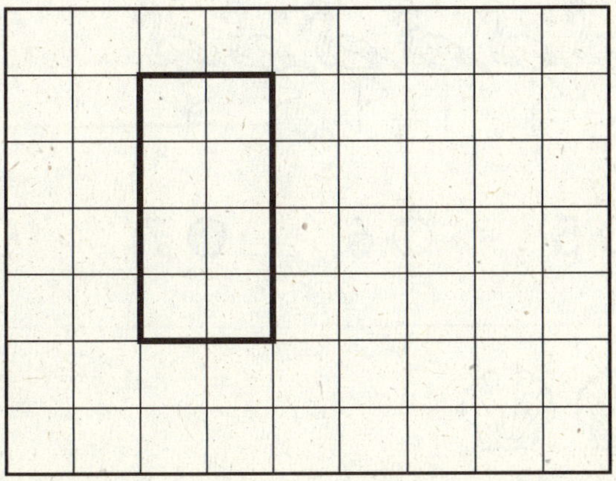

○ 5 ○ 6 ○ 7 ● 8

6.

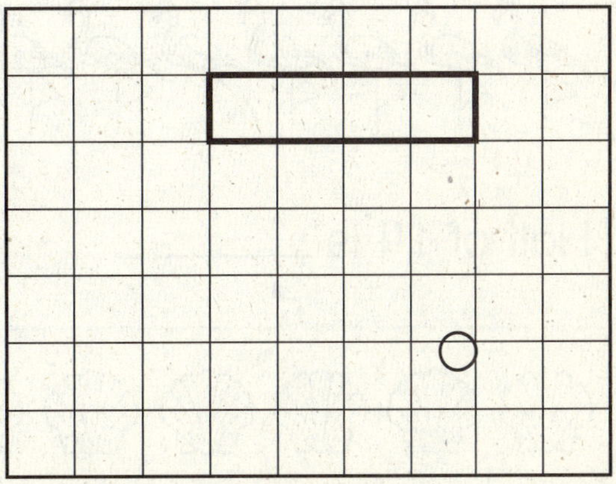

○ 5 ● 4 ○ 3 ○ 2

How much is shaded?

7.

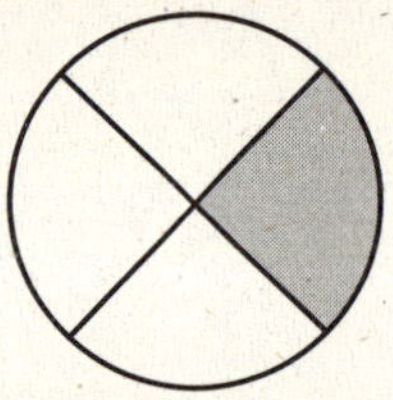

- ○ $\frac{1}{2}$
- ○ $\frac{2}{1}$
- ● $\frac{1}{4}$
- ○ $\frac{4}{1}$

8.

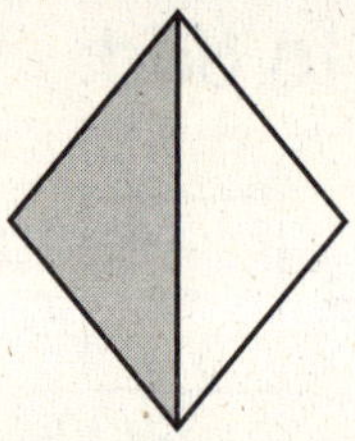

- ● $\frac{1}{2}$
- ○ $\frac{2}{1}$
- ○ $\frac{1}{4}$
- ○ $\frac{4}{1}$

9.

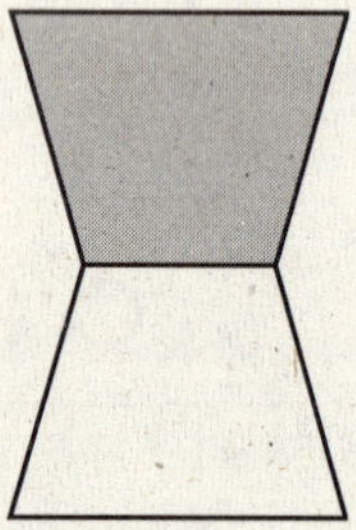

- ● $\frac{1}{2}$
- ○ $\frac{2}{1}$
- ○ $\frac{1}{4}$
- ○ $\frac{4}{1}$

Find one half of the objects. Then choose the best answer.

10.

Half of 14 is ______. ○ 5 ○ 6 ● 7 ○ 8

11.

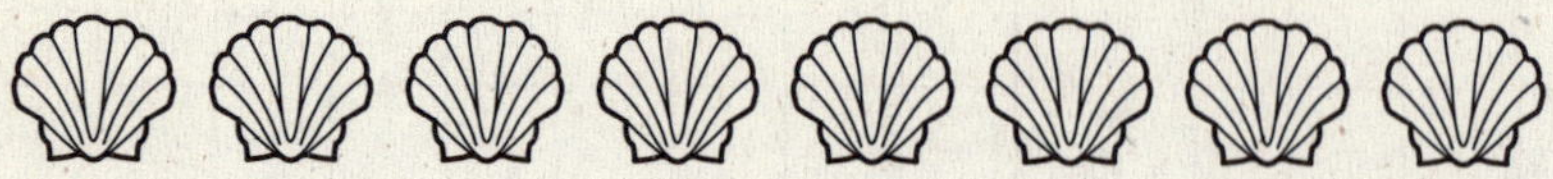

Half of 8 is ______. ○ 2 ○ 3 ● 4 ○ 5

Name

Find one fourth of the objects. Then choose the best answer.

12. 

One fourth of 4 is _____. ○ 1 ○ 2 ○ 3 ○ 4

13. 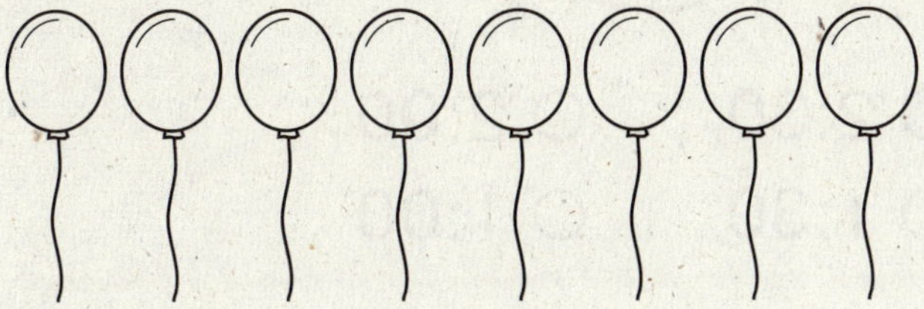

One fourth of 8 is _____. ○ 1 ○ 2 ○ 3 ○ 4

Use the circle graph to answer the questions.

Animals at the Aquarium

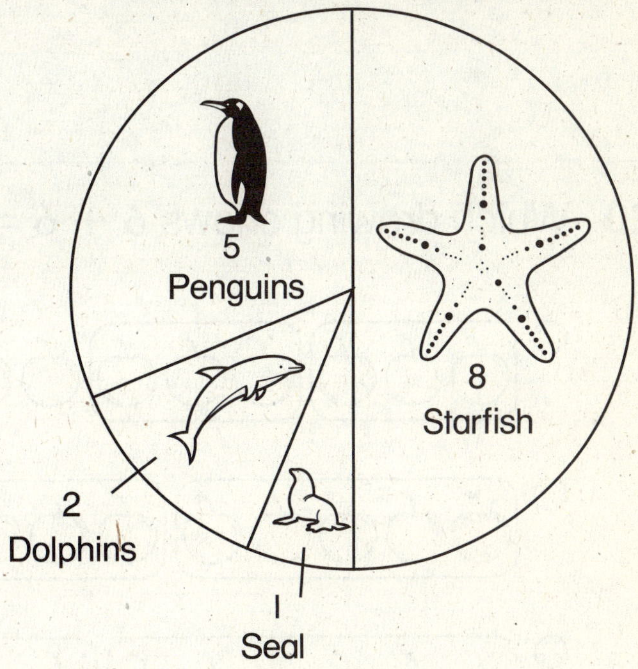

14. The aquarium has the most of which animal?

○ Penguins
○ Seals
○ Starfish
○ Dolphins

15. How many more penguins are there than dolphins?

○ 1 ○ 2
○ 3 ○ 4

16. How many fewer seals are there than dolphins?

○ 1 ○ 2
○ 3 ○ 4

Name

What time does the clock show?

17.

- ○ 6:00
- ● 6:30
- ○ 7:00
- ○ 7:30

18

- ● 2:30
- ○ 2:00
- ○ 1:30
- ○ 1:00

---

19. Which month comes after January?

- ○ December
- ● February
- ○ March
- ○ November

---

20. Which drawing shows 6 + 6 = 12?

○ 

○ 

● 

○ 

Fractions, Circle Graphs, and Clocks

What Is Assessed

- Find one half and one fourth of a geometric figure.
- Find lines of symmetry.

Explaining the Assessment

1. Read the task with the class. Let children know that you are available to help them if they have difficulty reading any of the instructions.

Materials

Tracing paper, scissors

Possible Responses

Question 1: Children divide the rectangle into halves horizontally, vertically, or diagonally. Some may draw a curved line.

Question 2: halves

Question 3: Check children's work.

Question 4: Explanations will vary. Children should recognize that in a symmetrical figure, both parts are mirror images of one another.

Name ______________________________

ACTIVITY Cutting in Half

1. Draw a line to show how each of these rectangles can be cut into 2 equal parts. Each line must be different.

2. Did you make halves or fourths? ______________

3. Ring the rectangles that show a line of symmetry. Use tracing paper and scissors to help you decide.

4. How can tracing and cutting help you to see if a rectangle has a line of symmetry?

Performance Assessment Rubric

An Exemplary Response (4 points)

- Draws lines to clearly divide shapes into halves
- Correctly names halves
- Identifies shapes with a line of symmetry
- Uses mathematical language and diagrams to explain how to check whether a line is a line of symmetry

A Proficient Response (3 points)

- Draws lines to divide shapes into halves
- Correctly names halves
- Identifies a shape with a line of symmetry
- Uses mathematical language or diagrams to explain how to check whether a line is a line of symmetry

An Acceptable Response (2 points)

- Draws lines that approximate dividing a shape into halves
- Correctly names halves
- Identifies a shape with a line of symmetry
- Provides some criteria for deciding whether a line is a line of symmetry

A Limited Response (1 point)

- Draws lines that approximate dividing a shape into halves
- May correctly name halves
- May identify a shape with a line of symmetry
- Does not provide reasonable criteria for deciding whether a line is a line of symmetry

Unit 8
Quick Quiz 1

Name ____________________

Show the price with sticks and circles.
Write how many of each coin.

1. 

Dimes 5   Nickels 1   Pennies 1

2. 

Dimes 7   Nickels 1   Pennies 4

How many cents?

3. 

43 ¢

4. 

22 ¢

Name ____________________

Add the numbers. Make a proof drawing with sticks and circles.
Did you make a new ten?

1. 27
+ 52
79

New ten?
☐ yes
☑ no

2. 65
+ 17
82

New ten?
☑ yes
☐ no

3. 35
+ 24
59

New ten?
☐ yes
☑ no

4. 71
+ 19
90

New ten?
☑ yes
☐ no

5. 15
+ 46
61

New ten?
☑ yes
☐ no

Unit 8
Quick Quiz 3

Name ______________________________

Solve the story problems.

Show your work. Use drawings, numbers, or words.

1. Javier bought pens for 2 dimes, 3 nickels, and 4 pennies. How many cents did he pay? 39 ¢

pen

2. Curtis paid 6 dimes, 2 nickels, and 1 penny for a pretzel. How many cents did he pay?

71 ¢

pretzel

3. Sandra bought a book for 4 dimes, 4 nickels, and 6 pennies. How many cents did she pay? 66 ¢

book

4. Stephen bought a pack of markers for 7 dimes, 3 nickels, and 3 pennies. How much did he pay? 88 ¢

marker

5. Lisa paid 2 dimes, 1 nickel, and 6 pennies for a basketball. How many cents did she pay? 31 ¢

basketball

Name ______________________

How many cents?

1. 

10 10 10 10 1 1

42 ¢

2. 

10 10 10 10 10 5

55 ¢

How much altogether? Solve with sticks and circles.

3. 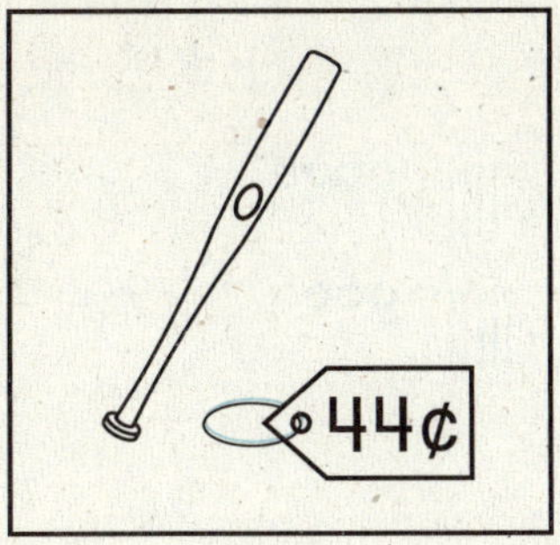

+ 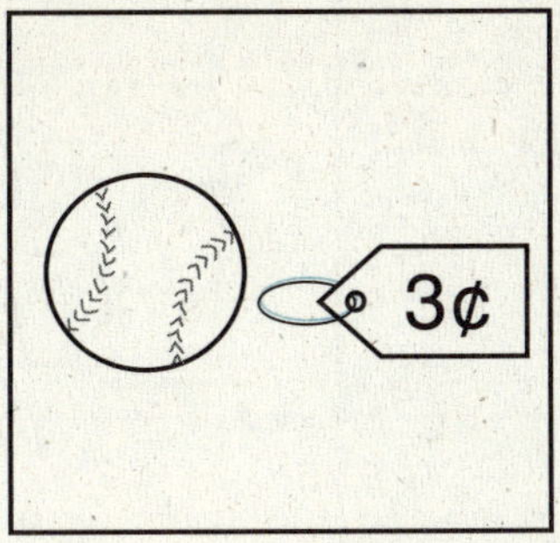

47 ¢

Name

Add the numbers. Make a proof drawing with sticks and circles. Did you make a new ten?

4.

$$\begin{array}{r} 52 \\ +\ 22 \\ \hline 74 \end{array}$$

New ten? ☐ yes ☑ no

5.

$$\begin{array}{r} 46 \\ +\ 35 \\ \hline 81 \end{array}$$

New ten? ☑ yes ☐ no

6.

$$\begin{array}{r} 28 \\ +\ 13 \\ \hline 41 \end{array}$$

New ten? ☑ yes ☐ no

7.

$$\begin{array}{r} 44 \\ +\ 53 \\ \hline 97 \end{array}$$

New ten? ☐ yes ☑ no

Name

Solve the story problems.

Show your work. Use drawings, numbers, or words.

8. Albert bought a new fish for his fish tank for 4 dimes, a nickel, and 2 pennies. How many cents did he pay?

[47] ¢

9. Stephan paid 6 dimes and 8 pennies for a pair of scissors. How many cents did he pay?

[68] ¢

10. Extended Response Add 54 and 27. Did you make a new ten? Explain.

Check children's work.

Name ______________________

Fill in the ○ for the correct answer.

How many cents?

1. 

○ 32¢ ● 47¢ ○ 52¢ ○ 60¢

2. 

○ 24¢ ○ 27¢ ○ 43¢ ● 53¢

How much altogether?

3. 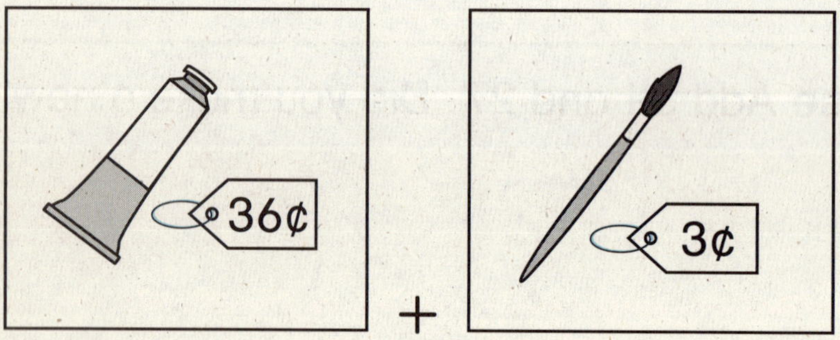

○ 35¢
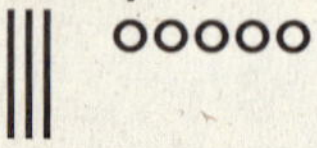

○ 38¢

● 39¢

○ 61¢

Name

Add the numbers.

4. 29 + 13

○ 16 ○ 36 ● 42 ○ 52

5. 28 + 62

● 90 ○ 88 ○ 80 ○ 72

6. 11 + 55

○ 44 ○ 46 ○ 65 ● 66

7. 37 + 14

○ 23 ○ 43 ● 51 ○ 52

Name ______________________________

Solve the story problems.

Show your work. Use drawings, numbers, or words.

8. Kate bought a bottle of water for 7 dimes, a nickel, and 2 pennies. How much did she pay?

bottle

○ 37¢ ● 77¢
○ 82¢ ○ 95¢

9. Paul found coins in his pocket. He had 4 dimes and 7 pennies. How many cents did he find?

pocket

○ 11¢ ● 47¢
○ 57¢ ○ 74¢

10. Add 79 and 19.

○ 60 ○ 68 ○ 88 ● 98

Money and 2-Digit Addition

What Is Assessed

- Find money amounts.
- Add two 2-digit numbers with and without regrouping.
- Make change for 1 dollar with 2-digit coin amounts.

Explaining the Assessment

1. Ask if children have visited a yard sale or flea market. Ask those children who have to tell about what they saw at the sale, and how much it cost.

2. Read the task aloud to the children. Let children know that you are available to help them if they have difficulty reading any instructions.

Materials

Real or play money (dimes, nickels, and pennies)

Possible Responses

Question 1: Children draw two different groups of coins, each with a value of 25¢.

Question 2: Children should ring items with a total cost less than $1.

Question 3: Children should show coins, or write a money amount equal to the cost of the items in Question 2.

Question 4: Children should show coins, or write a money amount equal to the difference between the cost of the items in Question 2 and $1.

Name ______________________________

ACTIVITY Sale

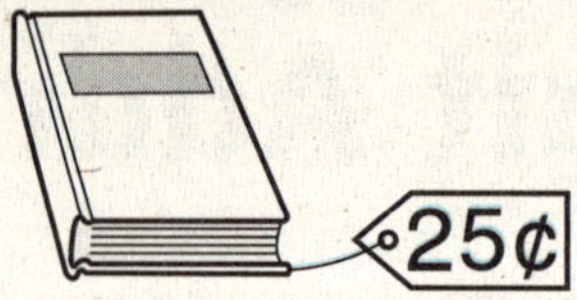

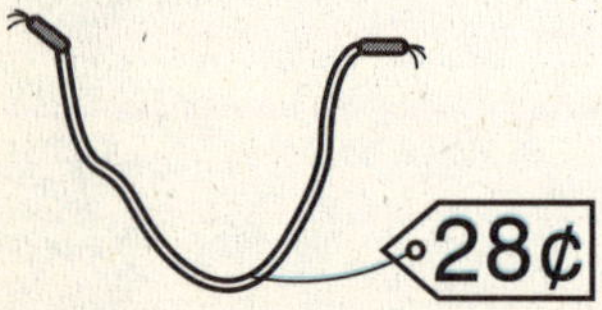

1. Draw coins to show the amount you need for 1 book. Then draw coins to show the amount another way.

2. You have 1 dollar to spend at the sale. What will you buy? Ring the things you will buy.

3. How much will you pay? ______________

4. How much money will you have left over? How do you know?

Performance Assessment Rubric

An Exemplary Response (4 points)

- Accurately represents money amounts as coins and with numerals
- Adds 2-digit numbers correctly and efficiently using any method
- Accurately calculates change for a dollar
- Clearly explains method used to make change for a dollar

A Proficient Response (3 points)

- Accurately represents money amounts as coins and with numerals
- Adds 2-digit numbers accurately, using any method
- Calculates change for a dollar with few or no errors
- Explains method used to make change for a dollar

An Acceptable Response (2 points)

- Sometimes represents money amounts accurately as coins and with numerals
- Adds 2-digit numbers with few errors
- May make significant errors in calculating change for a dollar
- Partially explains the method used to make change for a dollar

A Limited Response (1 point)

- May not represent money amounts accurately as coins or with numerals
- Adds 2-digit numbers with several errors
- May make significant errors in making change for a dollar
- May not explain an effective method for making change for a dollar

Unit 9
Quick Quiz 1

Name ______

Solve the story problems.

Show your work. Use drawings, numbers, or words.

1. Jasmine found 6 rocks. Ethan found 5. How many rocks did they find together?

rock

[11] rocks
label

2. Peter made some cards. Lakia made 5 cards. They made 16 cards in all. How many cards did Peter make?

card

[11] cards
label

3. Stan collected 7 leaves. Then he found 8 more leaves. How many leaves did he have in all?

leaves

[15] leaves
label

4. Stacy drew a flag with 14 stripes. 10 were red and the rest were blue. How many stripes were blue?

flag

[4] stripes
label

Unit 9
Quick Quiz 2

Name ______________________________

Solve the story problems.

Show your work. Use drawings, numbers, or words.

---

1. The store sold 12 red trucks and 5 yellow trucks. How many trucks did it sell?

truck

[17] trucks
label

---

2. Jenna has 20 blue marbles and 7 orange marbles. How many marbles does she have?

marble

[27] marbles
label

---

3. Terrel counted 14 buildings. There were 5 banks and the rest were shops. How many were shops?

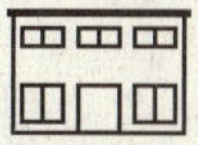
building

[9] buildings
label

---

4. In the garden there are 14 tomatoes and 23 carrots. How many vegetables are in the garden?

carrots

[37] vegetables
label

Unit 9
Quick Quiz 3

Name ______________________

Solve.

1. 8 − 2 + 3 = 9

2. 30 + 20 + 7 = 57

Solve the story problems.

Show your work. Use drawings, numbers, or words.

3. 8 people were on the elevator. Then 4 people got off and 3 people got on. How many people are on the elevator now?

people

7 people
label

4. Sally picked 6 oranges. She gave 4 away. Then she picked 9 more. How many oranges does Sally have now?

orange

11 oranges
label

Name ____________________

Solve the story problems.

Show your work. Use drawings, numbers, or words.

---

1. Ryan planted 12 sunflowers in the garden. Eve planted 4 sunflowers and 6 tulips. How many sunflowers did they plant in all?

tulip

[16] sunflowers
label

---

2. The store has 6 blue sweaters, 3 black sweaters, and 5 brown jackets. How many sweaters does the store have?

sweater

[9] sweaters
label

---

3. In the park Scott saw 7 black dogs, 14 oak trees, and 3 yellow dogs. How many dogs did Scott see?

dog

[10] dogs
label

Unit 9 Test
Form A

Name ______________________________

Solve.

1. $8 - 4 + 3 =$ [7]

2. $60 + 20 + 3 =$ [83]

Solve the story problems.

Show your work. Use drawings, numbers, or words.

3. Yesterday, Jamie picked 23 lemons. Today he picked some more. He picked 56 lemons in all. How many lemons did he pick today?

lemon

[33] lemons
label

4. There were 28 ducks. Some ducks flew away. Now there are 19 ducks left. How many ducks flew away?

duck

[9] ducks
label

Name

Solve the story problems.

Show your work. Use drawings, numbers, or words.

5. The store sold 31 bicycles and 11 skateboards. How many toys did it sell?

bicycle

42 toys
label

6. The forest has 26 trees. 4 are birch trees and the rest are elm trees. How many elm trees are there?

tree

22 elm trees
label

7. In a book, James saw pictures of 4 black bears, 2 elephants, and 3 brown bears. How many bears did he see?

bear

7 bears
label

8. Selma had 6 red crayons, 5 blue crayons, and 3 yellow crayons. How many crayons did she have in all?

crayon

14 crayons
label

Name

Solve the story problems.

Show your work. Use drawings, numbers, or words.

people

9. There were 8 people in line for the ride. 5 people left and 2 more people got in line. How many people are in line now?

[5] people

label

10. Extended Response Write a story problem. Solve it.

*Item 10 also assess the Process Skills of Problem Solving and Communication.

Name ______________________________

Fill in the ○ for the correct answer.

Solve.

1. $9 - 4 + 5 = \square$

○ 9 ● 10
○ 11 ○ 12

2. $30 + 40 + 5 = \square$

○ 65 ○ 74
● 75 ○ 345

Solve the story problems.

Show your work. Use drawings, numbers, or words.

3. Yesterday, Pat found 37 leaves. Today she found some more. She found 61 leaves in all. How many leaves did she find today?

leaves

○ 13 leaves ● 24 leaves
○ 51 leaves ○ 61 leaves

4. There were 34 carrots. Some of the carrots were eaten. Now there are 15 carrots left. How many carrots were eaten?

carrot

○ 11 carrots ● 19 carrots
○ 29 carrots ○ 49 carrots

Name

Solve the story problems.

Show your work. Use drawings, numbers, or words.

5. The store sold 41 sneakers and 25 sandals. How many shoes did the store sell?

sandal

○ 16 shoes ● 56 shoes
○ 58 shoes ○ 66 shoes

6. There are 16 books on the shelf. 9 are reading books. The rest are math books. How many are math books?

book

○ 5 books ● 7 books
○ 15 books ○ 25 books

7. At the pet store James saw 4 brown dogs, 7 orange cats, and 8 black dogs. How many dogs did he see?

cat

○ 4 dogs ○ 11 dogs
● 12 dogs ○ 15 dogs

8. The store has 8 corn muffins, 4 bran muffins, and 6 blueberry muffins. How many muffins does the store have?

muffin

○ 10 muffins ○ 12 muffins
○ 14 muffins ● 18 muffins

Name

Solve the story problems.

Show your work. Use drawings, numbers, or words.

9. There are 15 people on the train. Then 4 people get off and 9 people get on. How many people are on the train now?

people

○ 28 people ● 20 people

○ 12 people ○ 10 people

10. There are 6 children playing on the swings. There are 3 children playing on the slide. There are 5 adults reading. How many children are playing?

slide

○ 8 children ● 9 children

○ 11 children ○ 14 children

Unit 9

Analyze Story Problems

What Is Assessed

- Solve teen number story problems with unknown partners and totals.
- Solve category story problems with unknown partners and totals.
- Solve multiple-step story problems.
- Write story problems.

Explaining the Assessment

1. Show children 8 counters. Count them together. Place 6 in a small open box or basket. Ask how many are in the box, how many are out of the box, and how many there are altogether.
2. Tell children that farmers keep track of their animals. To keep them safe they need to know where they are on the farm.
3. Read the task aloud with the class. Let children know that you are available to help if they have trouble reading any of the instructions.

Materials

Counters

Possible Responses

Question 1: 13 cows in all, 9 sheep in, 6 pigs out, 11 ducks in all

Question 2: Answers may vary.

Question 3: Story problems and solutions may vary.

Name ____________________

ACTIVITY Animals at the Farm

Some animals are in the barn. Some are out.

1. Find the unknown partners or unknown totals.

4 cows in 9 cows out _____ cows in all	_____ sheep in 7 sheep out 16 sheep in all
6 pigs in _____ pigs out 12 pigs in all	3 ducks in 8 ducks out _____ ducks in all

2. Complete the story problem.

__________ kittens were in the barn.

Then __________ more came into the barn.

Then __________ went out.

How many are in the barn now? __________ kittens

3. Write a story problem about the farm.

Solve it. Show your work.

Performance Assessment Rubric

An Exemplary Response (4 points)

- Solves all single-step teen number problems correctly
- Completes and solves multiple-step story problems correctly
- Writes mathematically challenging story problem (for example, using teen numbers or more than one operation) and solves it correctly

A Proficient Response (3 points)

- Solves all single-step teen number problems correctly
- Completes and solves multiple-step story problems correctly, or with minor errors
- Writes a story problem and solves it correctly

An Acceptable Response (2 points)

- Solves most single-step teen number problems correctly
- May have one or more errors in solving a multiple-step story problem
- Writes and solves a story problem with minor errors

A Limited Response (1 point)

- Solves some single-step teen number problems correctly (may find totals correctly, but not partners)
- May have one or more errors in the solution to a multiple-step story problem
- May write a story problem and not provide a solution, or may write a very simple story problem (for example 2 ducks in and 2 ducks out)

Name ______________________

Estimate how many inches. Then measure and write the length.

1. 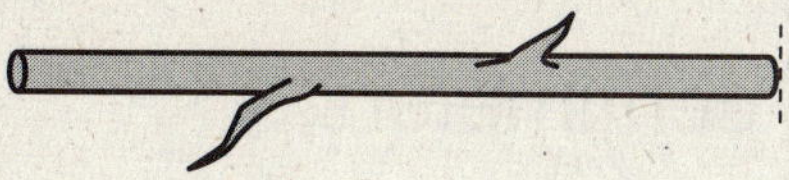

Estimate: about [ ] inches   Measure: [2] inches

Estimate will vary.

2. 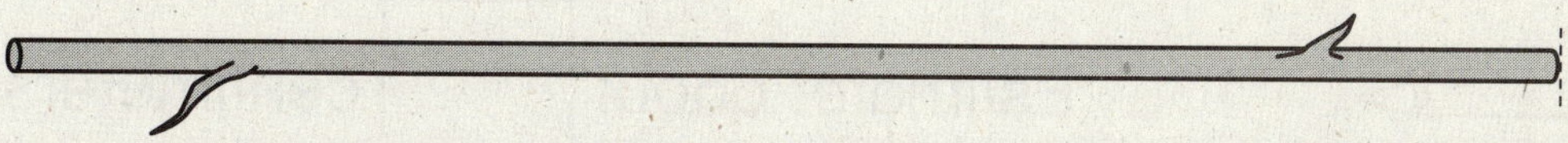

Estimate: about [ ] inches   Measure: [5] inches

Estimate will vary.

Measure the shape. Round to the nearest inch.

3. 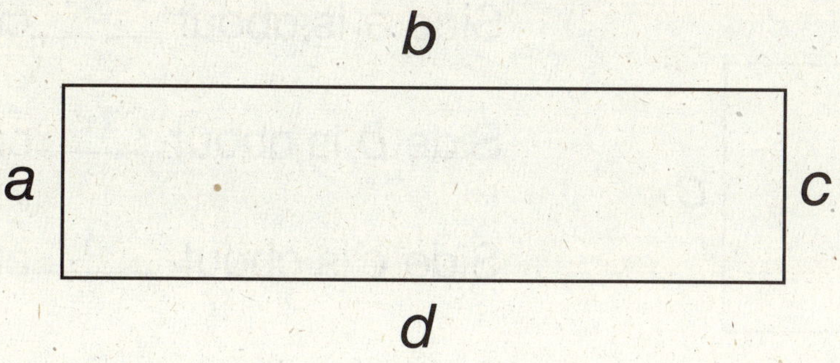

Side *a* is about __1__ in.

Side *b* is about __3__ in.

Side *c* is about __1__ in.

Side *d* is about __3__ in.

Use an inch ruler.

Measure the length and width of the rectangle below.

4. 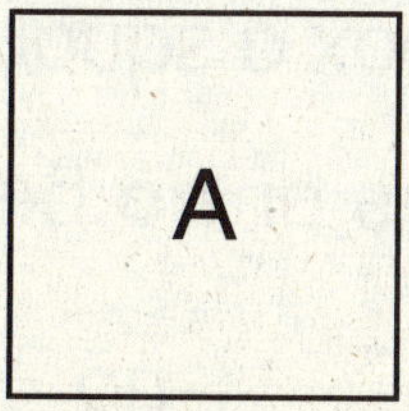

Length = __1__ in.

Width = __1__ in.

5. Is the box a square?

Ring **yes** or **no** below.

(yes)   no

Unit 10
Quick Quiz 2

Name ______________________________

Estimate how many centimeters. Then measure and write the length.

1. 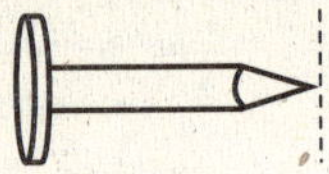

Estimate: about [ ] centimeters

Estimate will vary.

Measure: [2] centimeters

2. 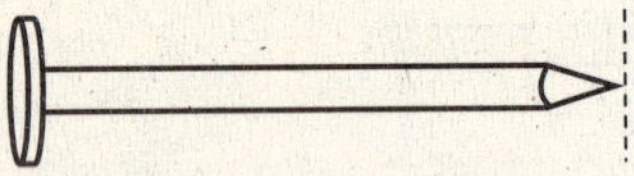

Estimate: about [ ] centimeters

Estimate will vary.

Measure: [4] centimeters

Measure the shape. Round to the nearest centimeter.

3. 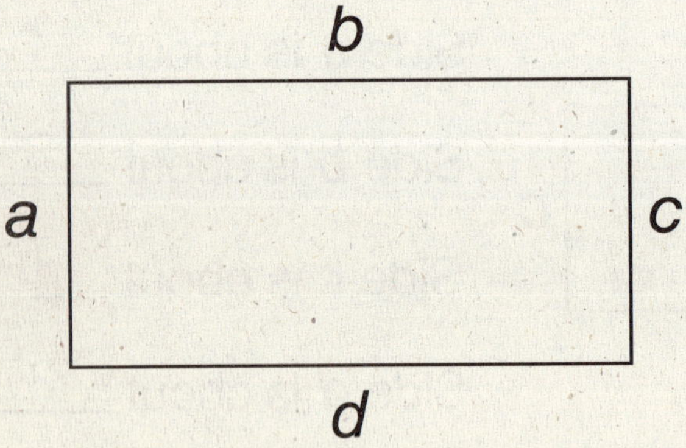

Side *a* is about __3__ cm.

Side *b* is about __6__ cm.

Side *c* is about __3__ cm.

Side *d* is about __6__ cm.

Use a centimeter ruler. Measure the length and width of the rectangle below.

4. 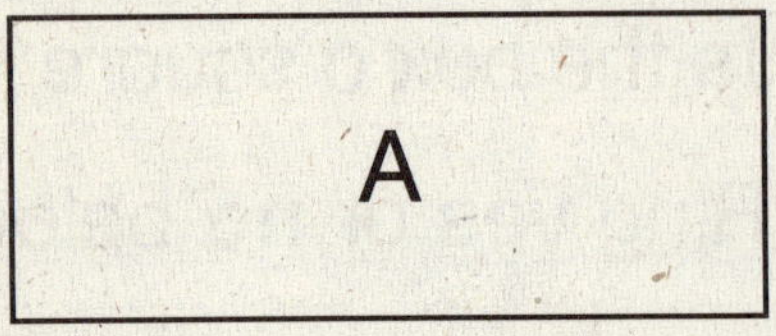

Length = __5__ cm Width = __2__ cm

5. Is the box a square?

Ring **yes** or **no** below.

yes (no)

Unit 10
Quick Quiz 3

Name ______________________________

Ring one group of ten. Estimate about how many in all.
Count to check. Estimates will vary.

1.

Estimate	Actual Count
	35

2.

Estimate	Actual Count
	27

Ring the measuring tool you use.

3. How much it holds?

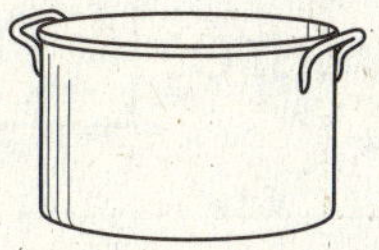

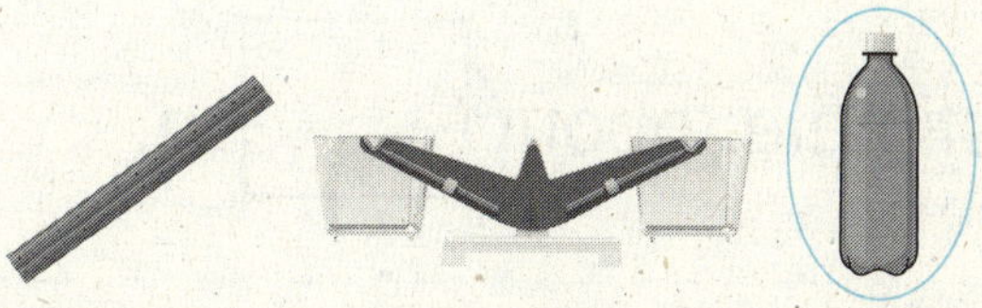

---

4. How heavy?

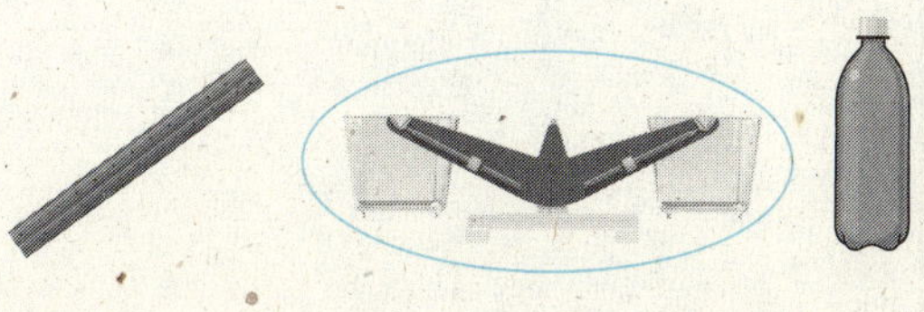

Name ____________________

Estimate how many inches. Then measure and write the length.

Estimates will vary.

1. 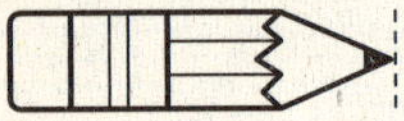

Estimate: about ☐ in. Measure: 1 in.

2. 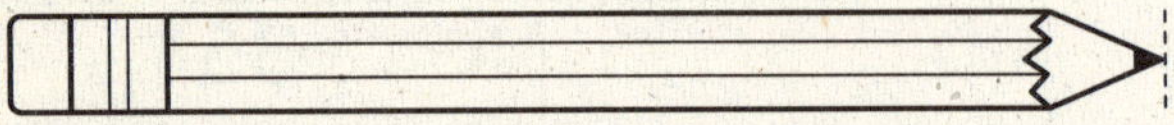

Estimate: about ☐ in. Measure: 3 in.

3. 

Estimate: about ☐ in. Measure: 5 in.

4. 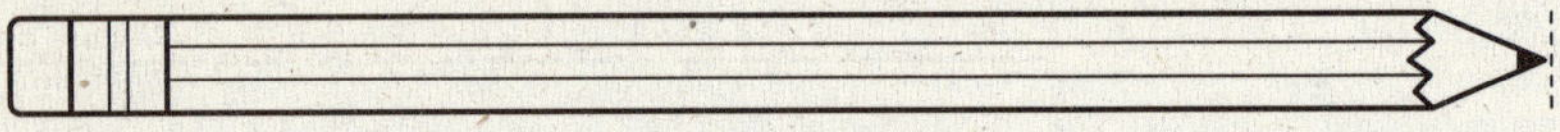

Estimate: about ☐ in. Measure: 4 in.

5. 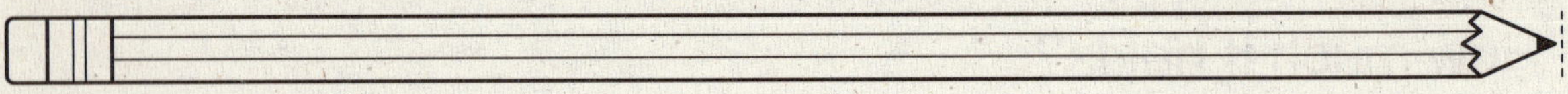

Estimate: about ☐ in. Measure: 6 in.

Measure the shape. Round to the nearest inch.

6. 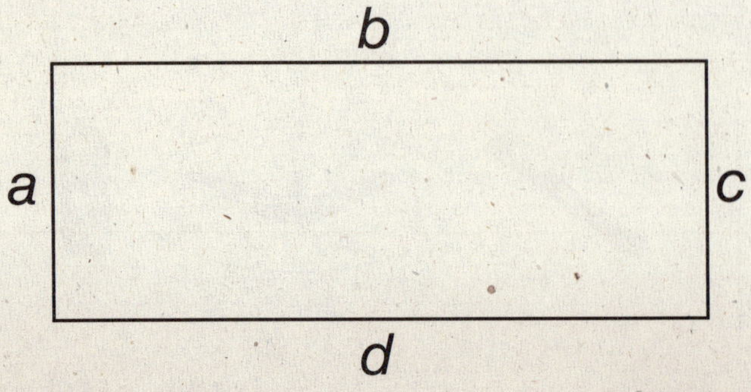

Side *a* is about 1 in.

Side *b* is about 3 in.

Side *c* is about 1 in.

Side *d* is about 3 in.

Name

Use an inch ruler. Measure the length and width of each rectangle.

7.

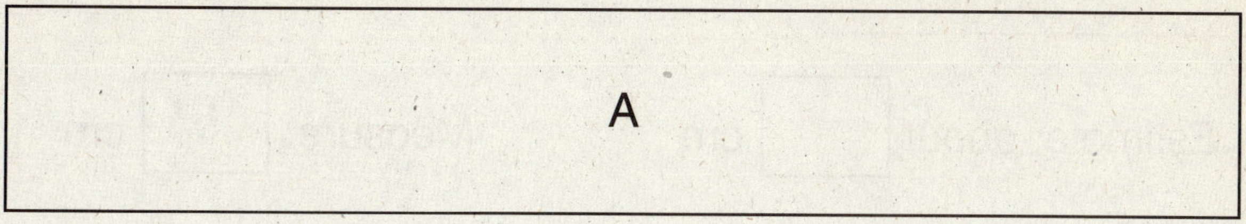

length = 6 in. width = 1 in.

8.

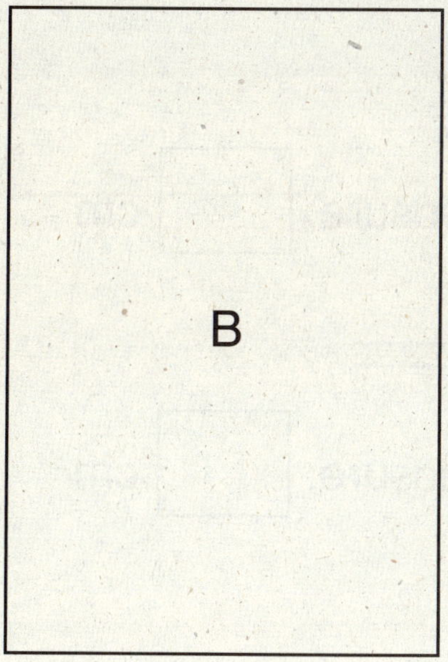

length = 3 inches

width = 2 inches

9.

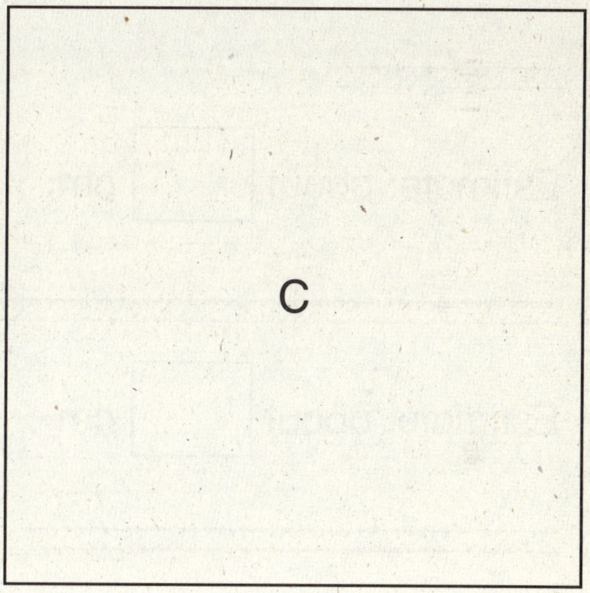

length = 3 inches

width = 3 inches

10. Look at shapes A, B, and C above. Which shape is a square?

Ring the letter below.

A B C

Name ______________________________

Estimate how many centimeters. Then measure and write the length.
Estimates will vary.

11. 

Estimate: about ☐ cm   Measure: 5 cm

12. 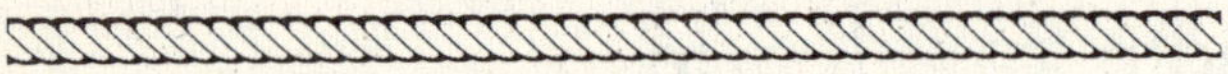

Estimate: about ☐ cm   Measure: 8 cm

13. 

Estimate: about ☐ cm   Measure: 3 cm

14. 

Estimate: about ☐ cm   Measure: 11 cm

15. 

Estimate: about ☐ cm   Measure: 7 cm

Measure each side. Round to the nearest centimeter.

16. 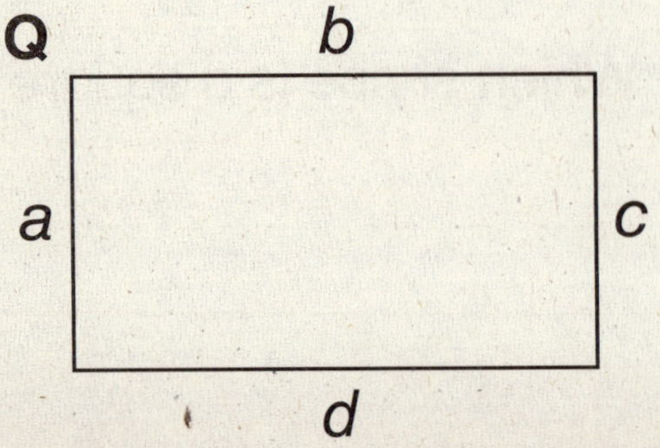

Side *a* is about 3 cm.

Side *b* is about 5 cm.

Side *c* is about 3 cm.

Side *d* is about 5 cm.

Name ______________________________

Use a centimeter ruler. Measure the length and width of each rectangle.

17.

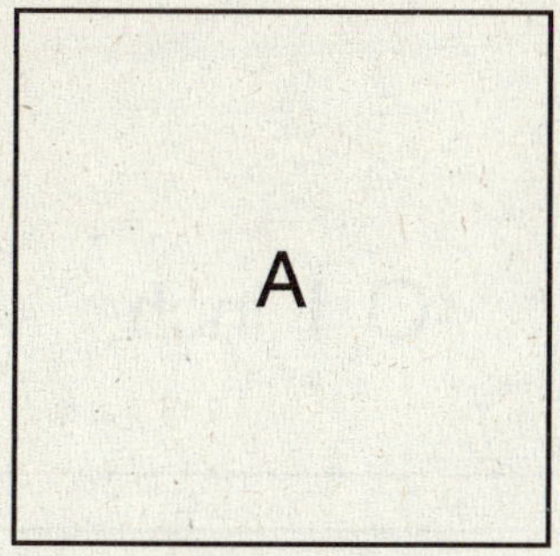

length = 4 cm

width = 4 cm

18.

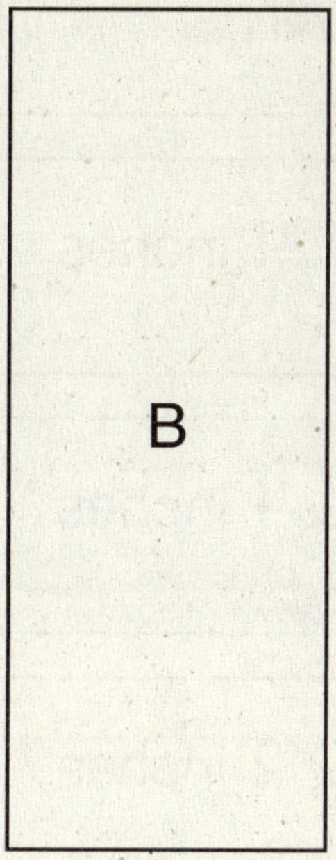

length = 8 cm

width = 3 cm

19. Look at shapes A and B above. Which shape is a square?
Ring the letter below.

(A) B

20. **Extended Response** How can you measure to find if a rectangle is a square?

Check children's work.

Unit 10 Test
Form B

Name ______________________________

Fill in the ○ for the correct answer.

Use an inch ruler. Measure to find the length.
Then choose the answer.

1. 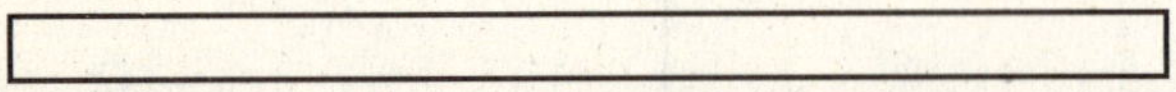

○ 5 inches ○ 4 inches ● 3 inches ○ 1 inch

2. 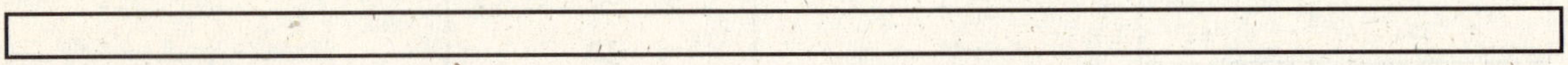

○ 3 inches ○ 4 inches ○ 5 inches ● 6 inches

3. 

○ 1 inch ○ 2 inches ○ 3 inches ● 4 inches

4. 

○ 6 inches ● 5 inches ○ 4 inches ○ 3 inches

5. 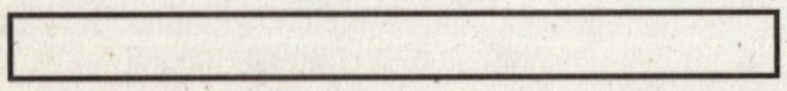

● 2 inches ○ 3 inches ○ 4 inches ○ 5 inches

Measure side *c*. Round to the nearest inch.

6. 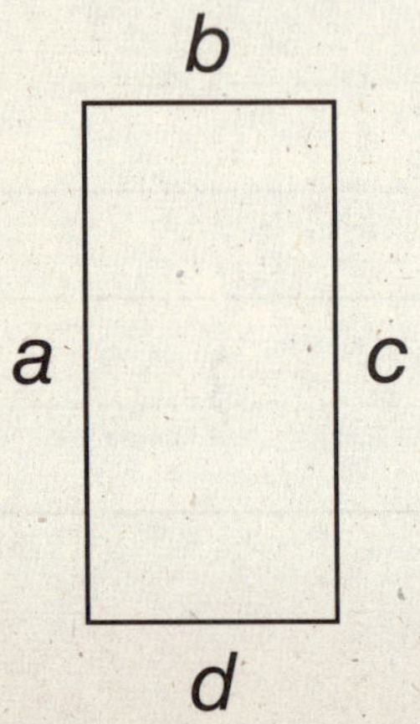

○ 1 in.

● 2 in.

○ 3 in.

○ 4 in.

Name

Use an inch ruler.

Choose the measurements that match each rectangle.

7.

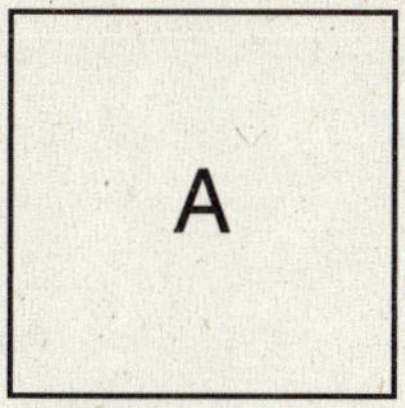

○ Length = 2 inches   Width = 2 inches

○ Length = 2 inches   Width = 1 inch

● Length = 1 inch   Width = 1 inch

○ Length = 1 inch   Width = 2 inches

8.

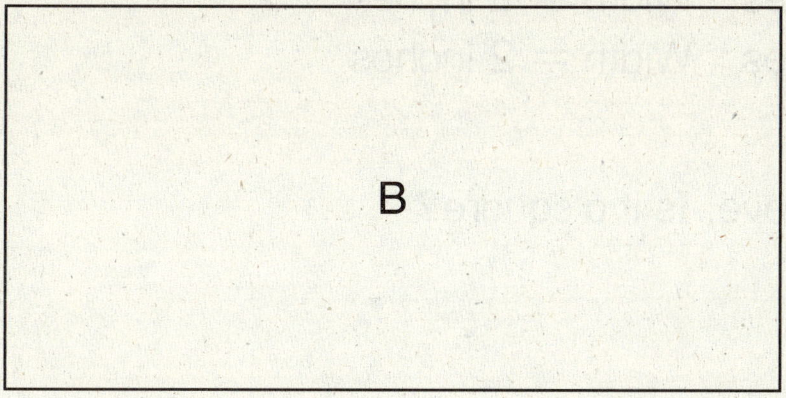

○ Length = 4 inches   Width = 3 inches

○ Length = 2 inches   Width = 4 inches

● Length = 4 inches   Width = 2 inches

○ Length = 2 inches   Width = 3 inches

Name

Choose the measurements that match each rectangle.

9.

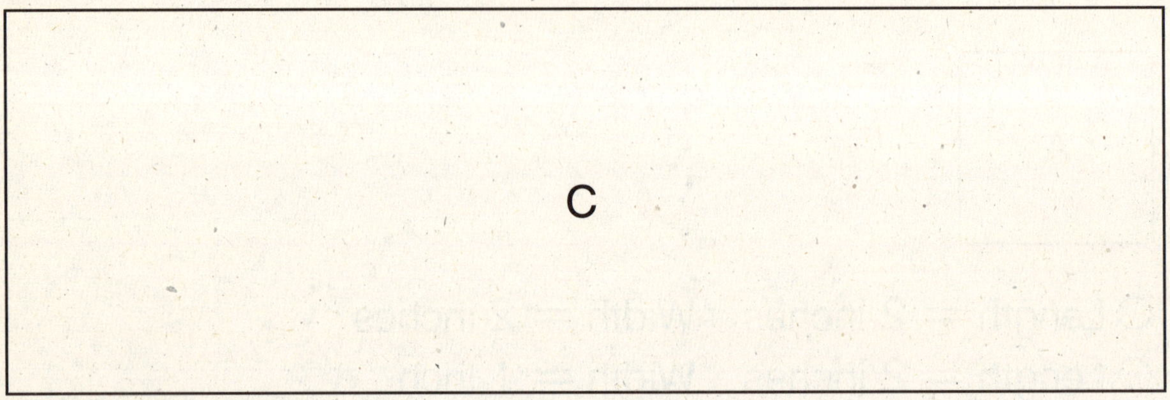

○ Length = 6 inches Width = 1 inch
○ Length = 2 inches Width = 6 inches
○ Length = 5 inches Width = 2 inches
● Length = 6 inches Width = 2 inches

10. Look at shape C above. Is it a square?

● no ○ yes

Name ______________________________

Use a centimeter ruler. Measure to find the length.
Then choose the answer.

11. 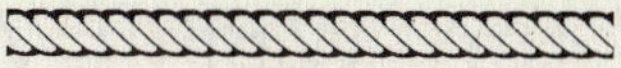

○ 2 cm ○ 3 cm ● 4 cm ○ 5 cm

12. 

○ 6 cm ● 7 cm ○ 8 cm ○ 9 cm

13. 

○ 9 cm ○ 10 cm ○ 11 cm ● 12 cm

14. 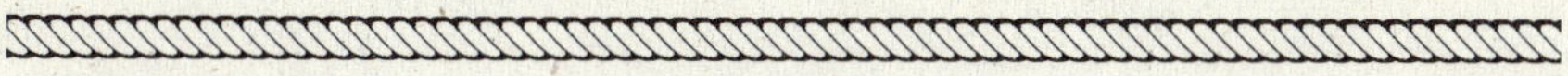

○ 10 cm ● 11 cm ○ 12 cm ○ 13 cm

15. 

● 3 cm ○ 4 cm ○ 5 cm ○ 6 cm

Measure side *a*. Round to the nearest centimeter.

16. 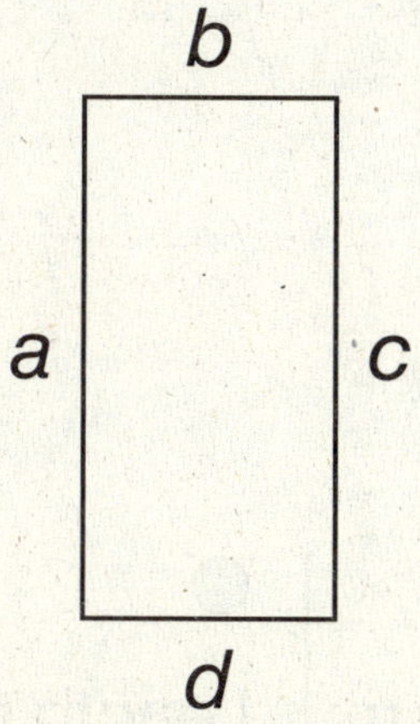

● 4 cm
○ 3 cm
○ 2 cm
○ 1 cm

Name ____________________

Use a centimeter ruler. Choose the correct measurements.

17.

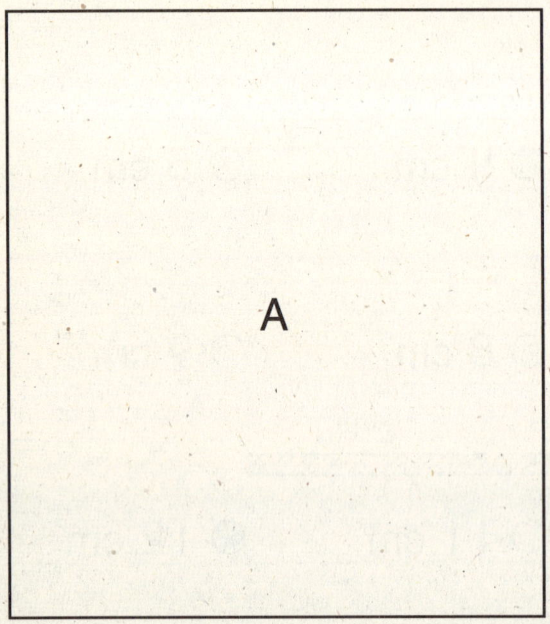

- ○ Length = 7 cm Width = 8 cm
- ○ Length = 7 cm Width = 7 cm
- ● Length = 8 cm Width = 7 cm
- ○ Length = 8 cm Width = 6 cm

18.

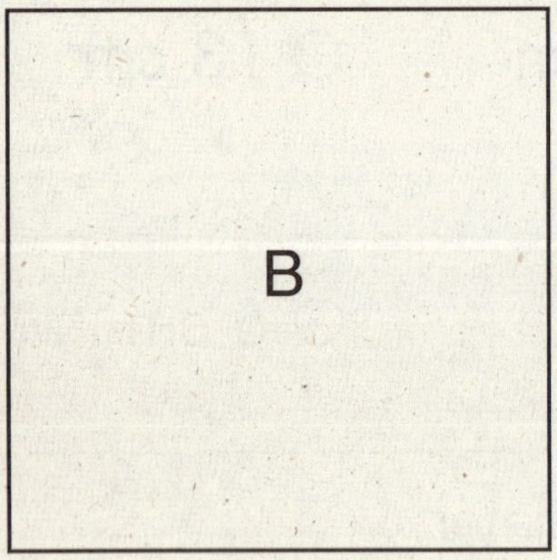

- ○ Length = 4 cm Width = 4 cm
- ○ Length = 5 cm Width = 3 cm
- ○ Length = 5 cm Width = 4 cm
- ● Length = 5 cm Width = 5 cm

19. Look at shape B above. Is it a square?

○ no ● yes

20. Which of these measurements is a square?

○	○	○	●
Length = 2 cm	Length = 6 cm	Length = 5 cm	Length = 5 cm
Width = 3 cm	Width = 4 cm	Width = 1 cm	Width = 5 cm

Unit 10

Measurement

What Is Assessed

- Estimate and measure length in inches.
- Estimate and measure length in centimeters.
- Estimate length using nonstandard units.

Explaining the Assessment

1. Talk with the class about some lengths in the classroom. Ask children to suggest how they could measure them.
2. Read the task aloud to the children. Let children know that you are available to help them if they have difficulty reading any instructions.

Materials

Inch ruler

Centimeter ruler

Variety of small items to use to measure, including paper clips

Possible Responses

Question 1: Estimates will vary. The bed is approximately 3 paper clips long (if using standard-sized paper clips).

Question 2: Estimates will vary. The bed is 3 inches long.

Question 3: Estimates will vary. The bed is approximately 8 centimeters long.

Question 4: Drawings will vary. Each child's measurement should match his or her drawing.

Question 5: Answers will vary.

Name ____

ACTIVITY Busy Bug's Bed

This is Busy Bug's bed.

1. How long is Busy Bug's bed? Use a paperclip.
   Estimate. Then measure.

   Estimate: about ______ paperclips

   Measure: about ______ paperclips

2. How long is Busy Bug's bed in inches? Estimate. Then measure.

   Estimate: about ______ in. Measure: ______ in.

3. How long is Busy Bug's bed in centimeters? Estimate. Then measure.

   Estimate: about ______ cm Measure: about ______ cm

4. Busy Bug has a sister. Draw her bed. Then measure her bed.

5. Whose bed is longer? How do you know?

Performance Assessment Rubric

An Exemplary Response (4 points)

- Makes reasonable estimates in non-standard units, inches, and centimeters
- Measures accurately to the nearest whole unit with non-standard units, inches, and centimeters
- Writes all measurements with appropriate units
- Correctly identifies longer bed
- Uses mathematical language to clearly explain how he or she knows one bed is longer than another

A Proficient Response (3 points)

- Makes reasonable estimates in non-standard units, inches, and centimeters
- Measures accurately to the nearest whole unit
- Writes all measurements with appropriate units
- Correctly identifies the longer bed
- Uses some mathematical language to explain how he or she knows one bed is longer than another

An Acceptable Response (2 points)

- Makes reasonable estimates using at least two of non-standard units, inches, and centimeters
- Measures accurately to the nearest unit in most cases
- Writes some measurements with appropriate units
- Correctly identifies the longer bed
- Explains how he or she knows one bed is longer than another; may not use mathematical language

A Limited Response (1 point)

- May include two or three estimates that are unreasonable
- May include several inaccurate measurements
- Writes few or no measurements with appropriate units
- May correctly identify longer bed
- May include partial explanation of how he or she knows one bed is longer than another

